STANDING TALL
FROM THE
INSIDE

STANDING TALL

FROM THE INSIDE

Angie Clucas

First published in 2020 by Dean Publishing
PO Box 119
Mt. Macedon, Victoria, 3441
Australia
deanpublishing.com

Cataloguing-in-Publication Data
National Library of Australia
Title: Standing Tall From The Inside
Edition: 1st edn
ISBN: 978-1-925452-23-5
Category: Memoir/self-help/juvenile non-fiction

This is an autobiography, the author has tried to recreate events, locales and
conversations from her memories of them. In order to maintain anonymity
of certain individuals in some instances names, occupations and places have
been changed to protect individuals. Certain identifying characteristics and
details such as physical properties, occupations and places of residence may
have changed.

This book is a personal memoir and not intended as a substitute for the
medical advice of physicians. The reader should regularly consult a physician
in matters relating to his/her health and mental health particularly with
respect to any symptoms that may require diagnosis or medical attention.
This is not intended for medical purposes or promote any particular type of
treatment than that recommended to the individual from their own medical
team — each person is different.

The views and opinions expressed in this book are those of the authors and
do not necessarily reflect the official policy or position of any other agency,
publisher, organization, charity, medical team, employer or company.

Assumptions made in the analysis are not reflective of the position of any
entity other than the author(s) — and, these views are always subject to
change, revision, and rethinking at any time. The authors or organizations
are not to be held responsible for misuse, reuse, recycled and cited and/or
uncited copies of content within this book by others.

PREFACE

When we are children, we learn things at a very high rate, and the lessons we learn come by making mistakes, and by playing, and by testing our boundaries.

One of the first things we learn is that adults are the ones who have the control, but that they are also the ones who should guide us to survive the many different aspects of living in this world.

Living in this world isn't always easy, in fact, it can be very challenging.

My life is dedicated to making the journey of life easier for others. And trust me, with the right advice, support and guidance, it does get easier.

"First they ignore you, then they ridicule you,
then they fight you, and then you win."

Mahatma Gandhi

To my daughter, Silvia.

*Having you was the proudest
moment of my entire life.*

"Every moment is a fresh beginning."

T.S. Eliot

CONTENTS

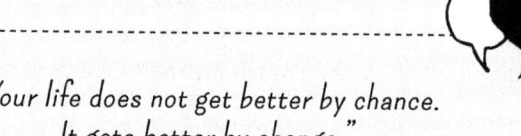

"*Your life does not get better by chance.*
It gets better by change."

Jim Rohn

INTRODUCTION

My name is Angela Clucas. I was born in Christchurch and grew up in Darfield, on the South Island of New Zealand. When I was born on 11 May 1969, my birth weight was 2 lb, 6 oz, or around 1kg, and I was less than 30cm in length. To put that in a visual, I weighed about the same as a tub of margarine and was about the same length as a school ruler.

I have lived my whole life being smaller than my peers and therefore, have had to deal with many issues around people not understanding why I am an abnormal height for my age. This has always been the case, as I was born with Russell-Silver syndrome (RSS). More on that later.

I'm writing this book not as a professional author, but as someone that has been bullied all my life. To this day, I still deal with bullying issues on a regular basis just because of my appearance. The people who do the bullying don't see the person I am within — the character, the soul, the whole person that is me. They just see someone different, someone small. But as Shakespeare once said, "and though she may be but little, she is fierce."

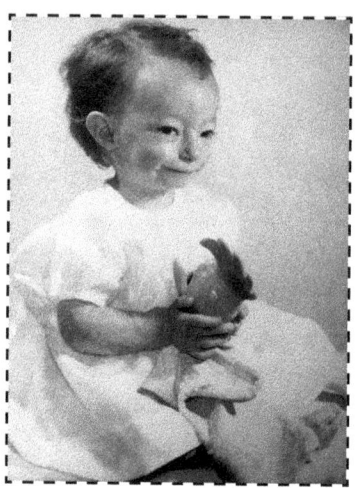

My main goal in life is to help others that suffer from being bullied. I want to show you that you don't have to think of being bullied as the end of any chance of a happy life. And although the focus of this book is on bullying and how to deal with it, to provide some meaning around my own lifelong experience with bullying, I want to first share with you some background into my life and living with RSS.

WHAT IS RUSSELL-SILVER SYNDROME?

Russell-Silver syndrome (RSS), also called Silver-Russell syndrome (SRS), is a growth disorder occurring in approximately 1/50,000 to 1/100,000 births. It is one of 200 types of short stature conditions in humans and one of five of these types that results in a smaller body size in all stages of life beginning from before birth.

The average adult height for females with RSS is 4'7" (139.7cm) and 4'11" (149.8cm) for males. Its exact cause is unknown, but present research points toward a genetic component. My 'tallest' adult height is 137cms or approx 4'5". I reached that height at 25 years of age and have been the same since. I wear size 12 children's clothing and shoes because no adult sizes fit me. It can be hard to find something that looks age-appropriate but still fits me. I'm not one for short frilly skirts or hot pink polka-dot dresses.

LIVING WITH RSS

Living with Russell-Silver syndrome is full of challenges and in my case, I've been told, these started from before I was even born.

I had some difficulty eating from a very young age, one of many symptoms of RSS. When I was young, food didn't interest me and feeding me as a child was a mission. I remember some days thinking that if we didn't have to eat, life would be so much easier and much less stressful.

Mum must have had to be so patient with me in my early days, just trying to make sure that I was getting the food I needed to survive: a harrowing thought. I've been told that sometimes it took an entire day to get even the minimum amount of food required into me. She has said that she was lucky that I was the first child and not her second or third, as she wouldn't have been able to spend as much time with me.

By the way, my brother and sister made up for me, they had no trouble eating their food! My siblings weren't born with RSS but I had no idea. By the time my brother could stand he was taller than me and three years younger, I actually thought he was taller because he was a boy.

But Russell-Silver syndrome comes with more than just being small. The left side of my body is slightly smaller than my right side, and it's much weaker. My left arm doesn't straighten fully and my left leg is much shorter than my right. My left shoe was always 'built-up' as a kid and I was never allowed to be barefoot; I always had to wear shoes. On the bright side, it helped me reach more stuff with that extra bit of shoe height.

My little fingers are bent and they will never be straight. It's my 'normal' and I'm used to it, except when I try to do things like typing class: I can only use four fingers and not five.

My mouth is small and I have too many teeth for my tiny jaw line, this resulted in an overcrowded bite, and in school my nickname became "Killer" because of this.

"If you think you're too small to make a
difference, you haven't spent a
night with a mosquito."
African Proverb

Growing up, my Mum and Dad treated me like any normal child, and for that I thank them. They never wrapped me up in cotton wool because of my small stature, and having their support made a big difference. But the challenges I was to face were inevitable.

Just learning the simple things like doing the dishes as a child was difficult because I was so tiny. I wasn't even able to reach the kitchen sink. Nevertheless, Mum would not make excuses for me. Instead, she would tell me to "go and get a kitchen chair, climb up on it, and do the dishes". Doing simple things like just reaching the tap to get a glass of water, I would have to get a chair to stand on. I became an expert at moving chairs around the house to reach objects.

Most people of normal height take things like having a shower for granted, but I had to always ask for help to turn the taps on and off. Even to this day as an adult, when I stay in hotel rooms there are challenges for me, especially if there are no chairs that are easy for me to move. I need chairs for things like getting cups out of overhead cupboards or reaching towels from a towel rack if the rack's above a bath. In fact, while we're on the subject, as an adult, having a shower over a bath in a motel or hotel room is my worst nightmare: I can't bloody reach the shower rose so if someone's moved it after I've organised it to be in the right position in the first place, I can't move it even standing on a chair, so the water goes all over the floor!

These sorts of challenges may seem relatively insignificant, even humorous if you look at them as one-offs but when dealing with them on a daily basis is your norm, it effects every part of your life. My experience of this started as a very young child but going to school presented a whole new list of things that I had to deal with, in a huge and often humiliating way.

Of the many examples I faced at school in these kinds of situations, the one etched in my memory as the most embarrassing of them all involved the fact that I wasn't strong enough to open a particular door — the main entry door into the school toilets. One day, when I was in there alone, I found myself stuck in the toilets because I couldn't pull the heavy door open to get back out.

Yep. I had to stay in the stinky toilets all by myself until someone found me. I had haunting visions of me spending the night all alone in the cold, dark stinky toilets. Luckily, the cleaner found me after school. But I had missed my school bus home. Mum had to drive all the way to school to get me, none of us were happy vegemites. From that day on, whenever I went to a new school I had to make sure I could open all the toilet doors before my first day. Can you imagine how embarrassing that was? But it was my reality and for safety reasons it had to be done.

The trials at school were continuous. In the classroom the tables and chairs were too big for me. This included the teacher's desk. When we had to line up to get our work marked, in my case I had to literally throw my work up and over, onto the teacher's desk because I couldn't reach it like the other kids. I also had to make sure I was one of the first in line so the pile didn't stack up too high. Luckily, I was always sitting at the front of the class, not too far to run to the teacher's desk. This was one of the only races I could win. Otherwise, the pile of workbooks to be marked grew too high for me to throw mine on top.

Travelling on the school bus was another challenge. We were always getting into trouble for having our shoes on the seat but sitting with my shoes on the seat was the only way I could sit comfortably. For a start, I had to climb up on to the seats just to sit down. Then, once I was up there, I couldn't reach the floor so, my legs were always hanging down. This wasn't very comfortable, so I used to sit cross-legged with my feet up on the seat as I had plenty of room, being so small.

I spent most of my time on the bus on the front seat alone because the drivers kept saying that they couldn't see me in the rear-view vision mirror if I went and sat with my friends. I felt like I was being punished for being short.

> *"I never gave up. I had to think outside the box to adapt and make it work somehow. I never wanted to be treated any differently from the others, so I spent a lot of my time working out how to do things differently."*
>
> **Angie Clucas**

As for sport, well that was another drama as most of the equipment was not suitable for my size. But I never gave up. I had to think outside the box to adapt and make it work somehow. I never wanted to be treated any differently from the others, so I spent a lot of my time working out how to use and do things differently. Whether that meant holding a softball bat further down the handle so that I could control it better — whatever it was I had to do to get along, I was going to do it.

It was hard work, but I managed to maintain this attitude moving forward. Then one day, there came a bit of relief.

As a gift on the night of my 13th birthday, Mum took me to indoor bowls, and for this I was and still am so grateful. At last there was a sport that didn't require me to find new ways to use the equipment. All I had to do was learn the rules and get along with older people. Not very hard! Hooray!

I became very good at this game. So good, I managed to travel around the country playing indoor bowls as a rep for my local district. I learnt a lot about people skills during this time. I also met many wise people who gave me great advice that I still use to this day.

I got through my early teenagerhood like I did childhood, by using all of the resources I could muster. This set me up for the many more challenges that were to keep coming my way.

Learning to drive a car was another major test. They don't make cars for short people — as I was to find out — however, after putting a pillow behind my back, I was able to learn to drive. Thanks to my Dad, he taught me everything I needed to know and after a few weekend lessons, I was on my way, getting closer and closer to becoming independent. There was just one obstacle I still had to overcome and that was passing my driving test.

The first time I failed because the inspector felt I wasn't big enough to drive a car! Now that's the worst thing anyone can tell me: that I "can't" do something! That really gets my back up! So, I rebooked for the next week for a second go and to my surprise, this time his attitude towards me had changed. I passed by doing nothing different than the first time. I guess he finally discovered that short people can drive cars.

Only three months ago, in June of 2019, I finally bought a car for my 50th birthday, a car I can drive without a pillow behind my back. It's a red KIA Ceratopsian, and we all know red cars go faster. It's great to feel 'normal' driving and getting in and out of my car. No more messing around with seat covers to hold the bloody pillow in place. No more pillow. What a victory!

It's the little things in life that people take for granted that are challenges I live with every day. But having said that, I believe that living with Russell-Silver syndrome has contributed towards making me the person I am today.

This includes more personal strategies I use to stay strong, regardless of whether anyone else agrees or disagrees. For example, I don't look in the mirror, therefore, I never see what others see of my appearance. This helps me focus on what I feel from within. It helps being short because I can't see in most mirrors anyway, or I can only see the top of my head.

My character is much stronger and my outlook on life generally more positive than most people I encounter. I don't worry too much about what others think of me. If I did, I would have gone nuts a long time ago! I have developed a thick skin that helps me deal with people that lack education on how to approach people that are so called abnormal. Remember, 'normal' just means standard, typical, usual, common. Abnormal just means non-standard, atypical, unusual, uncommon. Neither means better, worse, good or bad.

The big message I have here in this introduction, is that I get most hurt not by kids, but by adults. Kids sometimes point at me, laugh in my face, call me names and think that I need to be told how short I am in case I didn't already know! But my hurt comes from the irresponsibility of the adults that are with them, when they fail to explain that these actions can cause lifelong damage to someone that has low self-esteem: that at any point in time when they are receiving these comments from strangers, it can be devastating.

I am lucky in a sense because I have lived with this all my life and was brought up by parents who taught me how to deal with my issues until I could work out my own way. If someone starts getting bullied a bit later in life, they may have no idea how to handle it. It is very confronting at first. You feel very alone because you don't know what to do, and unless you have that right person to talk to, the feelings can consume your life and your life goes downhill very quickly.

My main goal in life is to help others that suffer from being bullied. I want to show you that you don't have to think of being bullied as the end of any chance of a happy life.

There are so many lessons to learn from being bullied which can provide an opportunity to grow and develop your inner-strength and character and turn things around. Now, don't get me wrong. I'm not suggesting that being bullied is a good thing. It's not, it's horrible and demeaning and shouldn't happen to anyone. All I'm saying is that when I was bullied, I had to dig deep and discover some new inner resources and those resources have become a huge part of me and made me who I am today. Of course, you don't need to be bullied to develop them (that should never happen) but I suggest to people to begin to grow and use their mental and emotional strengths sooner rather than later because life is always unpredictable and you never know when you may need them.

There are ways to positively deal with situations that arise without lowering your standards as a person. Learning the skills to deal with bullies is the key to becoming the best person that you can possibly be as you come through and out the other side of these rough experiences.

Understand that when someone is being bullied, they are feeling very lonely and neither know what to do, nor what to say to others. People in this situation are facing these feelings night-and-day, every day and the longer they let these feelings build up inside without dealing with them, the bigger the problems become for them. Being bullied can make someone feel terribly isolated and alone. They can feel trapped and unsure how to deal with things.

"Tell someone about being bullied. This is the first step."

Angie Clucas

Finding someone to confide in will help a great deal because when you share your experiences with others, that's when problems can be resolved because people can't help you if you don't tell them. You just need to work out who could be the right person to talk to.

Is there anyone you can confide in? List
some possible 'right' people. They could be:
a parent, auntie or uncle, teacher, family
friend, grandparent, sports coach.

....

....

....

....

....

....

....

....

If you don't have anyone you can talk to...here are some amazing
professionals that you can talk to. They are experts and have heard
many bullying stories before. They can help you.

Kids Helpline have an awesome website that tells you what to do
if you're being bullied. They say "there's always something you can
do" and they list some good ideas:

- Keep your distance from a bully
- Don't bully them back
- Tell them what they are doing is not ok
- Talk to an adult you trust
- Take time to do something nice for yourself
- Have someone help you report cyberbullying or assault[1] (more
  on that in my upcoming chapters).

---

1   kidshelpline.com.au/teens/issues/bullying

YOUTH RESOURCES

- Kid's Helpline: kidshelpline.com.au
- Headspace: headspace.org.au
- Lifeline: lifeline.org.au
- ReachOut: au.reachout.com
- Beyond Blue: beyondblue.org.au
- Suicide Call Back Service: suicidecallbackservice.org.au

PARENT RESOURCES

- Dolly's Dream: parenthub.dollysdream.org.au
- National Centre Against Bullying: dollysdream.org.au/get-help

FIND YOUR OWN EINSTEIN

What's Einstein got to do with it?

Finding someone who inspires you can help you a lot when you are going through a tough time.

Albert Einstein was one of those people to me. He was known as a great scientist, but he also said some great things. And he was funny! Among his many wise sayings, ten in particular stood out to me.

The condensed versions in bold are quick reminders that I have taken as simple but powerful pieces of advice that I try to follow:

INSPIRATIONAL EINSTEIN

1. Follow your curiosity

"I have no special talent. I am only passionately curious."

2. Perseverance is priceless

"It's not that I'm so smart; it's just that I stay with problems longer."

3. Focus on the present

"Any man who can drive safely while kissing a pretty girl is simply not giving the kiss the attention it deserves."

4. Imagination is powerful

"Imagination is everything. It is the preview of life's coming attractions. Imagination is more important than knowledge."

5. It's okay to make mistakes
"A person who never made a mistake never tried anything new."

6. Live in the moment
"I never think of the future — it comes soon enough."

7. Create value
"Strive not to be a success, but rather to be of value."

8. Don't always expect different results
"If you want different results, you have to try different approaches"

9. Knowledge comes from experience
"Information is not knowledge. The only source of knowledge is experience."

10. Learn the rules and then play your best
"You have to learn the rules of the game. And then you have to play better than anyone else."

Whenever I find myself in a tough situation, stressed or upset, I go back to thinking about these lessons and that usually helps me make the best choices for myself instead of the wrong ones in the heat of the moment.

These are not the only wise sayings in the world, and Einstein is not the only inspirational figure in the world. You may find pearls of wisdom that you relate to from someone else entirely. It may be someone you know, or a famous person that has passed on like Albert Einstein. Or you may find it in someone you randomly meet.

My advice to everyone is to find your own lessons to live by so that when nasty issues arise you have something on hand to guide you to help you make good choices.

Having a role model or mentor, or someone you look up to can be really helpful when you're going through tough times.

WRITE AND REFLECT
Who do you look up to?

....

....

....

....

....

....

....

....

....

....

Who are some of your role models or people that inspire you?

....

....

....

....

....

....

....

....

....

....

Each chapter of this book includes my personal story and some of my favourite Einstein quotes related to the challenges I faced within each story. In reading these chapters and beyond, I hope you also take these two things into your heart:

1. Please treat others with the same level of respect that you wish to receive from others.

2. You must learn to live with the cards you are dealt with in life. And make the most of it. The choice is yours.

There is always a choice.

"During our lives we have to understand that when we are born we are given a name which becomes our identity. It is our life's responsibility to develop our character and to become a person of value in the community in which we live.
We must also understand that when we are born our parents don't get a instruction manual on how to bring us up. They do the best with what they have at the time."

Angie Clucas

"Life is a journey, not a destination."

Ralph Waldo Emerson

Chapter 1

MORE THAN YOUR NAME

"You are the person to save yourself because you understand yourself better than anyone else."

Angie Clucas

THE DREADED
SCHOOL BELL

My first day at school was a rude awakening, but not because of being woken up by my early morning alarm. This day marked the start of me having to deal with other people's reactions to me completely on my own. I wouldn't have the familiar comfort of Mum in the background to ask for help with anything that could arise during the day.

For the first time in my young life, I felt alone. I thought I'd be unable to handle others pointing their fingers at me and saying nasty words to me about my appearance. I suddenly felt very exposed to everything and was losing any confidence I thought I had. I did not like this big world they called school. I wasn't seeing it as fun or exciting, or anything else that people told me it would be like. All I was seeing were mean teasing children and nobody being at all friendly. Feeling very anxious and concerned, I couldn't help thinking, *I'm not going to survive this day*. Not to mention the many years ahead I had to be here, which looked like a forever nightmare.

When the school bell rang and it was time to go into our classroom, mentally things improved but physical obstacles already took their place. I had trouble climbing up onto my chair because it was too high, then once I had that problem worked out, I was faced with another drama: I couldn't see over the top of the chair to look at the blackboard at the front. This school thing was becoming a horror movie and I seemed to be the only person experiencing it like this.

I was trying to process so many issues that I wasn't even listening to the teacher. So, when she asked me a question, I switched on to autopilot and said, "I don't know". The question turned out to be "What's your name?" You can only imagine everyone's reaction to that and how stupid I felt.

During the next hour or so (and time was moving slow), life for me settled down a little, as all I had to do was sit there on my uncomfortable chair and listen to the teacher. Easy at last. Then, life changed again for the worse. The goddamn bell rang which meant it was morning teatime. This meant that I had to get off my chair without falling flat to the ground — a major challenge due to the fact that my feet were what felt like miles away from the classroom floor.

At morning tea, we had to go out to the hallway to get out our lunch boxes from our bags. The bags were on hooks and guess what! The teacher had put my bag on the hook for me and she was nowhere to be seen! I had to get my morning tea. I didn't yet know anyone in my class so there was no one that I could comfortably ask for help. *Where's that teacher?* I thought to myself. Adults are supposed to be there to help in these situations, I kept thinking, but at school this didn't seem to be the case. I started feeling a bit angry.

After a short time, I decided to get brave. I asked another kid to help me. They just walked off laughing, and I stood there getting angrier by the second. At this point, I decided it was up to me. I had to start dealing with these very frustrating issues. I looked around to see what I could move to stand on to help me reach my bag. I had already worked out that I only needed to get to the zip to open my bag and get my lunch box. So, the bag could stay on the hook. I dragged out a chair from the classroom, climbed up on to it, got my lunch box out and climbed back down. Mission accomplished.

Then, just as I found somewhere to sit and finally opened my lunch box, the school bell rang again! Morning teatime was over, and I hadn't even had a bite of food yet. I took some sultanas and started eating them on the way back to class. The teacher was at the door waiting for us, so I put my sultana packet in my pocket and asked her to help me put my lunch box back into my bag on the hook.

Once we were back in class, we had to sit on the mat, much to my relief. The teacher read us a story and we spent the rest of the class on the floor to my delight, issue free.

The bell rang again, letting us know it was lunch time, so I watched the teacher like a hawk so that I could ask her to help me with my lunch box. I wasn't getting caught out again. I was so hungry. Once we had all eaten our lunch, we were allowed to play. I decided that just sitting quietly would be the best thing to do. That way, nothing bad would be done to me. But that wasn't going to happen.

The other kids decided to go and get the pram that was supposed to be used for dolls. They come over, picked me up against my will and put me into the pram, to play with as their 'real-life baby'. I was totally shocked and had no idea how to deal with this new situation. I was really upset and the more I pleaded, "let me out of here", the worse the other kids' behaviour became towards me. In the end, I gave up and let them play their game. There was nothing I could do to stop them as there were too many of them and fighting to get out of the pram was going to make it worse.

When lunch was over and the bell was sounding to go back into class, the kids took off and I was just left sitting there, with no thought from any of them as to how I was going to get back to class. I then had to work out how to escape from the pram and make a run for the classroom, before I got into trouble for being late. Those students had no idea about the stress they had caused me.

My school life had not started favourably, to say the least. But I do remember thinking, *Well, I have to be at school for a very long time, so it looks like I'll have to put up with this all the time. I'm here now. How am I going to cope?* I knew I'd have to start dealing with it.

Over the next few days the kids continued to use me as their doll in the pram and I was really getting sick of it. So, I hatched a plan. One day, at lunch time before they could get to me, I went and climbed into the pram by myself and started eating my lunch. Now they couldn't pick me up to put me in the pram. I'd got some control back but needed to do more as they were still pushing me around.

I decided to get back at the boy that seemed to be the boss. While I was in the pram one lunch time, I said to him that I had "a secret" to tell him. My plan was to get him to come down to my level so that I could hit him in the face. Not the greatest plan in the world because

violence never resolves anything, and I wouldn't condone it now. But I was only 4 or 5 years old then and desperate to make my point.

The boy ended up with a bleeding nose and I got into trouble for it. When the teacher asked me why this had occurred, I got a chance to explain my feelings in front of everyone and as a result, the kids doing the bullying heard me and began to understand.

Once the students learnt that they were being very nasty and that their actions where having a damaging impact on my feelings, the whole thing suddenly stopped. After that, my life at school became a little less stressful. In fact, funnily enough, the 'boss' boy (who started it all) and I became best of friends.

> "When the teacher asked me why this had occurred, I got a chance to explain my feelings in front of everyone and as a result, the kids doing the bullying heard me and began to understand."
>
> **Angie Clucas**

I guess this incident taught me a few things:

1. Having someone understand what I was dealing with every day made a huge difference to my situation. I felt heard (but it shouldn't have taken an act of violence for this to occur).
2. Others understanding the impact that bullying had on me was important.
3. Finding new ways to deal with situations can have positive outcomes.

Now, of course, acknowledging bullying and calling out the behaviour doesn't always mean that it will stop and everything will be rosy. But, we must start educating young people on this subject early in order to stamp it out and not let it happen to others.

PERSEVERANCE IS PRICELESS

"It's not that I'm so smart; it's just that I stay with problems longer."

Albert Einstein

WRITE AND REFLECT

Did you know you can enter your answers straight in the interactive book and keep it for your eyes only? Go to **deanpublishing.com/angieclucas**.

Is there a situation (or someone) that you are dealing with right now and finding hard to cope with? Can you reach out to someone you trust (parent/teacher/family friend) and tell them about it? You can write what you would like to say here:

What does perseverance mean or look like to you? You should never have to persevere through a bully's behaviour but you can increase your perseverance in other areas like school, sports or playing an instrument.

....

....

....

....

....

....

....

List 3 situations where you've used your determination and how did you feel i.e. completing assignments, learning a new skill (sport, music, skateboarding, etc.).

....

....

....

....

....

....

....

STATING YOUR BOUNDARIES

We all have a little invisible circle around us called a boundary, it's like a force-field that you can't actually see but it exists. We all have the right to decide who we allow in to our inner circle boundary and who we don't allow in. It's important to have boundaries because good boundaries keep you safe. You are in charge of your boundary and you are the boss of who comes in and who stays out.

Only letting people you trust into your boundary is a good idea and leaving the people who make you feel bad out of your boundary is also a good idea. The good thing about being in charge of your boundary is that it's like a fence – you can decide when to erect it and when to drop it down. You can decide who comes in and out of your personal space.

If someone is being mean to you, it's okay to put your forcefield up and say "no". It's a brave thing to do. It's not always easy but your invisible forcefield is yours and it's there to protect you and keep you safe. This will help others understand that you have limits and boundaries and many people will respect you for it.

Sometimes people don't realise how bullying affects others. They don't understand or respect the fact that people have their own boundary. Some people are boundary bullies and always try to crash your fences down. Sometimes you have to put up your hand and say "no". Tell an adult if someone is repeatedly crashing your boundary and trying to interfere in your personal space.

Boundaries should be based on things and people that are important to you. For example, if you meet a new friend and you develop a trusting friendship you may like to allow them into your inner circle.

It's also okay to forgive people who are mean but that doesn't mean you have to accept them back into your inner circle. Your boundaries are yours, and yours alone. You decide.

Knowing your boundaries is helpful because it helps you decide what you will accept and what you won't accept. This will make it less likely for you to do something you're not comfortable with. For example, if someone is trying to manipulate you to take drugs or do something bad, they don't belong in your inner circle because they are not respecting you and trying to harm you.

YOUR BOUNDARY

You get to decide who goes in or out of your boundary

WHAT TO SAY IF PEOPLE CRASH YOUR BOUNDARIES

It's not always easy to put up boundaries but it is necessary when people don't respect them. You can say things like:

- "No!" - You always have the right to say "no". Saying a clear 'no' can take some practise but it's a powerful little word.
- "I'm not comfortable with this" or "This makes me feel uncomfortable."
- "I can't do that for you."
- "This doesn't work for me."
- "I've decided not to."
- "I'm not interested in doing that."
- "I don't want to do that."
- "I won't be joining you."
- "Back off!"

Remember to use confident body language as you speak (it helps strengthen your boundary).

- You can put your hand up like a stop signal.
- You can shake your head "no".
- Make direct eye contact.
- Use a clear tone of voice (not too soft, and not too loud).
- Stand tall with your head up.

Angie is sharing more in her INTERACTIVE book.

See exclusive, behind-the-scenes videos, audios and photos.

DOWNLOAD free content and learn how to live your best life.

deanpublishing.com/angieclucas

DEVELOP YOUR CHARACTER BUT DON'T LET THEM CHANGE YOU

From a person that has suffered my fair share of being bullied (mainly due to my appearance), I can say this: it's important to grow your own character. This doesn't mean you accept their behaviour at all, this just means you need to look after yourself, develop yourself and at times, even try to identify what makes a bully behave so terribly. Developing your character means to develop life skills that will help you be the best person you can be whilst also dealing with situations that pop up in life. Having a good character will help you when you met new circumstances and have to make decisions.

Developing your character can include things like:
1. Taking ownership of your own actions.
2. Having empathy for others.
3. Developing the ability to communicate, compromise and negotiate.
4. Expressing your feelings and wants with words rather than with impulsive behaviours or reactions.
5. Developing personal traits that support you like resilience, humour, determination and kindness.

Developing my own character not only made me a better person, it helped me deal with bullies and NOT become like them.

Use the lessons you've learnt through the experiences you have suffered or witnessed. Try to understand the other person's reasons as to why they lash out at certain people, remembering that there is always an underlying reason behind these types of actions.

Kids Helpline say that there are lots of reasons why someone might bully others but whatever the reason – it's never okay.

Someone who bullies another person might:
* Feel jealous
* Want others to like them
* Want to feel better about themselves
* Want to fit in with their friends
* Feel angry inside
* Like to be in control or have power over others
* Have been bullied themselves
* Not know what they're doing is wrong.[1]

As you get older, your brain starts to catalogue memories of these experiences, and you will become more skilled at dealing with different people when they behave in inappropriate ways. Now, of course, you shouldn't have to deal with people behaving badly at all but from all the people I have spoken to over the years, there seems to be a chronic problem of nasty people no matter what age you are or what country you live in.

I decided to start to build myself. To develop my own character and resilience. This way, I could tackle lots of different situations in life, not just bullies.

Learning simple skills like how to use your mindset, your emotions and your humour are wonderful skills to have in life in general. Don't change yourself to please others, only change yourself to become better than you were yesterday because YOU decide.

Don't let bullies change you. You are the one being kind and awesome and good. Don't let them make you believe that you are flawed or not good enough because that's not true. You are good enough just as you are.

When bullies picked on my appearance and hurt my feelings, I had to remind myself that they were the ones being awful and mean. That is being ugly from the inside. That's not cool. Abraham Lincoln said, "I would rather be a little nobody, then to be an evil somebody." I agree!

---

1 kidshelpline.com.au/teens/issues/bullying

Even celebrities get bullied these days. It's vicious and cruel. People who are talented and famous aren't out of the firing line, sometimes they cop it even more because others get jealous of their success. But the most interesting people are always unique. Embrace what makes you unique and don't let others change you.

One person I saw do this was young nine-year-old indigenous Australian boy Quaden Bayles. He was born with dwarfism and teased so badly at school one day that he was driven to despair. Someone sent me a video on Facebook that showed young Quaden crying his eyes out and wanting to die because he had been subjected to relentless bullying. His mum posted the video to draw awareness to the issue. It broke my heart watching him. I knew what it felt like to have a dwarfism condition so I reached out to him. I sent a video of myself to let him know he wasn't alone and I understood what being bullied was like. I don't know if he ever saw it, but what I do know is that something special happened. It wasn't just me that reached out to him, thousands of others did. From NRL football players to famous USA comedians and endless streams of kind people. He went from being teased and feeling alone to being supported from strangers all over the world. People gave lots of money to a Go-Fund-Me page for him, however Quaden's family didn't take the money, instead they asked for it to be given to charities. In a recent interview with National Indigenous Television (NITV) Quaden said, "If you get bullied, just stand up for yourself and don't listen to what they say." He also spoke about parents taking greater responsibility for educating their children about bullying and disabilities. He said, "The parents should make their kids be nice to people with disabilities."

I agree 100%. This young man is an inspiration and if we join his advocacy, and the many others that speak up and call out bullying, then one day, the bullies will stop! That is my dream: that no one gets bullied, ever.

> *"Falling down is part of life. Getting back up is character building for living."*
>
> **Angie Clucas**

FINDING YOUR WAY

Character and values are what shape us into the person we become, so why not use this as a platform to build your life. Start your journey by making a conscious decision to build a set of rules that you want to live by. And use this as a guide to help you navigate your way through whatever this world has in store for you.

As you go about your day-to-day life, you should remember that human contact is a big part of life so there is no way we can avoid dealing with others. Understanding and accepting this simple fact will help you when you are being tested by people that are not respecting you as an individual.

CREATING YOUR OWN RULES TO LIVE BY

It's important to make your own 'Rules to Live By' because it's your life and you are the one that needs to decide what will work for you and give you a wonderful future.

Rules are like an inner code that you hold yourself to. Having a strong set of rules makes it easier to make good decisions and move your life forward in a positive direction. Having my own set of rules helped me live with honesty and integrity and stopped me stooping to a low-level behaviour like the bullies.

Deciding what is most important to you may take time, and you may not be able to immediately make your 'Rules to Live By' list, but it's important to start thinking about it and writing down some notes.

HOW TO BRAINSTORM 'RULES TO LIVE BY'

1. Find a quiet place to sit and reflect. Take time to make it special for yourself.
2. Make a list of what is most important to you, what you value most.
3. Make a list of behaviours you admire and behaviours that you don't.
4. Decide what you want in the future and why you want it.
5. List things that are a "deal-breaker" to you (like being a bully to others or stealing).
6. Make rules that will steer your life in a positive and healthy direction.

Here are some examples of some people's lists:
- Be comfortable in my own skin
- Never bully another person
- Keep a positive attitude despite the odds
- Appreciate what I have and don't compare myself with others
- Think of five things I am grateful for every day
- Never take drugs or smoke
- Don't let toxic people into my circle
- Be kind to others.

Others include:
- Treat people the way you want to be treated
- Do a good deed every day.

WONDERFUL YOU

What do you like about yourself? Is it that you care, always have a smile for friends, you follow through and do something when you said you would?

....

....

....

....

....

....

....

How do you talk to yourself? What do you say about yourself in your head — are you kind and thankful and acknowledge your accomplishments or do you criticise yourself?

....

....

....

....

....

....

....

....

What are some helpful things you could tell yourself that would make you feel great?

....

....

....

....

....

....

....

....

....

How do you treat yourself? Are you kind to yourself when you mess up? Do you treat yourself the same way as your treat someone you respect?

....

....

....

....

....

....

....

....

Chapter 2

WRONG JOHN, NOT ON MY WATCH!

"Learning from your challenges becomes
part of your destination."

Angie Clucas

TIME TO
STAND TALL

I was in my last year of primary school and I'd got used to the fact that due to being short, others never gave me the time of day. One morning however, life was about to change forever. It is amazing how just having one new person added to the mix in a classroom can change everything.

What started out as just another ordinary day for me as a ten-year-old, turned out to be a very unusual day indeed. A day that would change how people would react to me from this day forward and I was completely unaware of what was about to unfold. The day started like any day: riding into school on my push bike, and then going to my first class for the day.

Sitting in class I would always take the row best for me to see the blackboard. And it was because of this vantage point, I was one of the first in the class to see the new student arrive. And this boy (we'll call him 'John', not his real name) really stood out. He was very tall and carrying a large amount of extra weight. He was almost the same size as some of the teachers in the school! Immediately I was thinking, *Great! Just what I need. More big people to stand over me and try to humiliate me.*

Actually, every student was shocked at the size of this kid. How could he be the same age as all of us? But as it turned out, John's size was not his only stand-out feature, unfortunately.

From the first words that came out of this boy's mouth, I felt that he'd have some major issues fitting into the class. He spoke with an abrupt attitude that none of us had ever had to deal with before. I worried that he would use his large size to push others around in order to get what he wanted; I had dealt with bullies before. As I sat there in class and watched his body language, my intuition said, *This is not going to be fun.* Meanwhile, the teacher told us that we had to make John 'feel welcome' and hang out with him at morning tea.

The morning teatime bell rang, we all got our lunch boxes and went outside. It was winter in New Zealand and if we lined up outside the staff room, we were able to buy a hot chocolate at morning tea. We lined up like usual to wait our turn, but John jumped in and started talking his way up the line. Within no time he was at the front of the line and was first to get his hot chocolate. No one said anything. I guess we were all trying to be nice to the new kid.

LEARN THE RULES AND THEN PLAY YOUR BEST

> *"You have to learn the rules of the game. And then you have to play better than anyone else."*
>
> **Albert Einstein**

Then, at lunch time we all played a game called 'four-square'. Four-square is a ball game using a rubber playground ball. The court is divided into four areas (squares), one for each player, and the ball is bounced back and forth between the players. A player is eliminated when a ball is bounced in a player's square and the player is unable to touch the ball into another player's square. The objective is to eliminate other players to achieve the highest rank on the court.

It was a game that the whole class played at lunch time every day. We all joined in.

On John's first day, he decided he didn't want to play but after a while, once we explained how the game worked, we talked him into playing with us. What a mistake that was!

John's version of playing four-square began by blatantly ignoring the rules, telling everyone that he wasn't 'out' when clearly, he was. But because he was so big, nobody wanted to stand up to him to tell him that he had to play by the rules like everyone else. John just continued playing by his own rules and didn't listen to anyone. He then started pushing people out of their squares so that he could be at the top of the rank and be the 'king'.

"Wrong John, this is not happening on my watch!" I said under my breath, I was so angry!

Finally, it was my turn to play. I was one square down from John and needed to come up with something quickly to try and eliminate him. So, I used my head (not literally) and put the ball down low in his square: my thinking was that he would take longer to get to the ball if it was lower and I could get him 'out'. The plan worked and John was out!

Of course, John couldn't accept that and started coming towards me to push me out, just like he'd done with every other kid that had got him out. But I was ready for John, and as he came towards me, I took a sidestep and instead of pushing me over, he fell onto the concrete and grazed his knee along with his nose. He seemed to fall hard because he was so big. It's a long way to fall when you're king!

Then, at that very moment, the bell rang to go back into class and the teachers came to get us, just in time to see the blood on John's knee and nose! So, questions had to be answered about what had occurred. I was ready to face the battle on my own like usual but then something completely unexpected happened.

Much to my amazement, the students that had been giving me a hard time up to now were the first to stand up for me! Jumping in, they told the teachers what had happened, but the teachers didn't believe them and instead, they asked John for his side of the story. He told a different story: in his version, I had picked on him and had organised a gang-up on him. His story was all about the rough treatment I had apparently dished out on him, and that it was all my fault. (The poor new kid!)

So, I was sent to the headmaster's office to do a 'please explain' which was a very new experience for me. I was told that I needed to be a kinder, more caring girl and they wanted me to be friends with John.

Well, John continued pushing around everyone in the class at every available opportunity and after a week, we'd all had enough. But I was the only one that had the guts to stand up to this boy. I had to try to make him understand that walking all over people was not going to help him fit into our class.

On the Monday of the next new week, I asked the class teacher to please come and watch us play four-square so he could see for himself what was happening. I thought with the teacher there, if we're lucky enough, John might just start playing by the rules.

Me having asked the teacher to come, did change our environment playing four-square but it didn't make any difference to John's behaviour. He just carried on, and now it was even worse because he was trying to get back at me for making him fall over in front of the whole class. He was out for revenge! This changed everything because the only way to stop him I worked out, was to stop playing four-square for a short period of time during which time hopefully, John would get over it. Unfortunately, that was not to be the case.

John started looking for me every lunchtime to try and push me over. But because he was so big and didn't move well, I had the advantage, and was always able to get away from him in time.

As it happened, John only lasted a few weeks in school and then he never came back, much to our whole class's delight! But it was a worthwhile experience for everyone involved. As a class we learnt some very valuable lessons that helped all of us: to pull together as friends even if you weren't friends before; that it's important to respect all class members; and that there is no need to be mean to each other.

> "This experience also taught me to never underestimate your own ability to stand up for what you believe in; and to always stand up for what is the right thing to do, remembering that you must always make sure you look at both sides of a story and be respectful to both sides."
>
> **Angie Clucas**

HOME LIFE AND BULLYING

Bullies aren't born bullies. Sometimes they become bullies because of things that are going wrong in their own life. For example, family breakdowns can create bullies, where kids start lashing out because of what's happening around them. They may be living in a bad home situation. And if they don't learn about acceptable social behaviours and boundaries at home, they think that behaving badly and bullying is normal behaviour.

A child will copy what they see others around them doing. When a child is being bullied by a parent or carer, chances are this is the behaviour they will learn, and carry out themselves. This is due to thinking that the adult who's 'caring' for them, knows how to act and behave, and that they are the role model to follow. Kids automatically accept that their parent or carer knows best. So, if a child learns that disrespect and abuse are normal behaviour because that's all they've been shown, that's how they'll start acting in public toward other people. They learn that this is the way to get power.

ANOTHER SIDE OF NORMAL

There is also the other side, that is, when a child is given too much power at home by getting anything and everything they want. This raises children who learn that there are no limitations, and that becomes their 'normal'. This means that, when they are in public and are told "no" for the first time, they have a meltdown, because they think that they are entitled to get everything they ask for. Suddenly, their power is taken away.

The child doesn't understand why this is as they've never been taught about limitations. A natural response, therefore, is to start being a bully, because they don't yet have the life skills required to deal with the small word "no". Unless taught otherwise, these children won't see their behaviour as bullying. They will think that it is normal, as this is how they've learnt to behave in their home environment.

BULLIES AREN'T BORN BULLIES

When a child feels that they are invisible in their own home they can sometimes start becoming a bully at school because they are trying to get attention so that someone notices them, even if it is for all the wrong reasons.

A child can see getting attention for doing bad things as great because at least someone is finally noticing them. It gives them a voice, a way to be heard. So, they develop the bad behaviour to get more attention: good or bad, it doesn't matter to them anymore.

When a child lacks love and attention at home, they start feeling they don't have a voice and that no one cares. It's a chain reaction which often involves feeling:

- Anger
- Sadness
- Resentment
- Depression
- Feeling unimportant as a member of their family
- Withdrawn.

As the Kids Helpline mentioned earlier, sometimes bullies might:

- Feel jealous
- Want others to like them
- Want to feel better about themselves
- Want to fit in with their friends
- Feel angry inside
- Like to be in control or have power over others
- Have been bullied themselves
- Not know what they're doing is wrong.

DIFFERENT TYPES OF BULLIES

There are different forms of bullies. Some are outgoing and aggressive and try to physically intimidate or hurt others. Some other bullies are more sneaky and shifty. These types usually do their bullying work in secret, like making up rumours or leaving people out of groups. Then there are other types of bullies that appear friendly and nice but they're actually fake and mean. These are the type that pretend to be a friend but then say nasty things behind other people's back.

Some bullies are more group bullies. They bully people when their friends are around because they feel important and strong. They pick on the weaker kid or make fun of the one not in the group. There are even serial bullies, bullies that go from one person to the next just trying to have someone they can control and intimidate.

I have met many of these styles and they are all bullies. They may have different 'styles' of bullying but it's still bullying. What's even worse is that some of these people grow up and continue to be bullies in the workplace or in sport or social settings.

POWERFUL WAYS TO BUILD SELF-ESTEEM

When your self-esteem is low, you tend to make bad decisions, like being friends with people who aren't nice to you. Some people let bullies into their lives as friends because they think they're the only ones who will be their friends.

But bullies try to destroy your self-esteem. Targeting the weak, bullies take their anger, hurt and frustration out on others to try and make themselves stronger. They will then encourage you to be like them. Bullies sometimes try to make you think that if you hurt someone else before they hurt you, then you will be the one in control and no one will hurt you again. This is a bully tactic and it's really nasty and weak because it's always about trying to make someone feel small and weak to make themselves feel strong. But in fact, it's the bullies doing the weak behaviour.

The lower your self-esteem becomes the less ability you have to operate your social skills effectively. This situation can deteriorate very quickly and if it does, you may begin a downhill spiral. This is when you find yourself in a very bad and sad time in your life.

If you've hit a place like 'this, a great way to start regaining your self-esteem, is to 'fake it until you make it'. You must start becoming confident with your social skills, and by practising you can achieve this, and your confidence will return.

Building your self-esteem also involves others; letting their positivity in and letting yours out. These three steps are a powerful start:

3 WAYS TO GET BACK GOOD SELF-ESTEEM

1. **Pat yourself on the back**
   Acknowledge you by patting yourself on the back and use positive self-talk when you have done something that helps or uplifts you or another.

2. **Allow others pat you on the back**
   Let others give you a pat on the back and say "Thanks". The aim is to stop you saying (out loud or in your head) "It was nothing" or "I didn't do much" and disempowering yourself.

3. **Be kind**
   Find something nice to say to someone every day. This will make both of you feel good. Everybody has their own superpower, but can you see it? Look deeper, what could you say to someone that would make their day?

Self-esteem building activities include doing helpful things for yourself and other people, and practising being more positive in general.

SELF-ESTEEM BUILDING ACTIVITIES FOR YOU

- Use positive words about yourself.
- Think positive thoughts about yourself.
- Do activities you like such as sports, hobbies, cooking, going camping, artwork or just playing with your pet.
- Smile more.
- Join a club with the same interests as you.
- Learn a new skill online: a foreign language, public speaking, yoga.

SELF-ESTEEM ACTIVITIES THAT HELPS YOU AND OTHERS

- Ask someone how their day is going.
- Praise others when they do something well or nice.
- Avoid criticising others.
- Ask if someone needs help.
- Be kind.
- Spend time with someone who needs it.
- Do an activity with family or friends.
- Help a charity or volunteer.

You are the only one that can decide to make changes in your actions. Take positive steps one at a time, it's not a race.

List 3 things you can give yourself a pat on the back for. It can be a small or big thing like being a good friend, finishing a project or being kind to your family.

....

....

....

....

....

....

....

....

....

List 3 times you've received a pat on the back from others. How did you feel?

....

....

....

....

....

....

....

....

....

List 3 times you've acknowledged others and praised them or given them a pat on the back.

....

....

....

....

....

....

....

....

....

....

....

THE POWER OF BODY LANGUAGE

Knowing how to use your body is important because body language is a form of communication. Both humans and animals use their body to communicate.

The forms of behaviour used in body language can be:

- Body posture
- Gestures
- Facial expressions
- Head nodding or shaking
- Eye movements.

Although body language is non-verbal or non-spoken, it plays a very important role in communication. It can also reveal your feelings and help you understand or read cues to how others may be feeling.

Think of how an animal behaves when they're scared, they can't tell you in words but you can understand that they are scared by the way that they act.

Having confident body language is a skill that anyone can learn. It helps you feel more confident and can prevent some bullies from trying to intimidate you.

Some things you can do to have confident body language:

- **Walk tall and hold your head high.** Yes, even if you're small like me, you can be tall on the inside and hold your body with certainty and respect. Using this type of body language sends a message that you're not vulnerable.
- **Eye contact** — look people in the eye. This shows that you are confident and not afraid (even if you have to fake it at the start...it gets easier).
- **Arms** — don't fold your arms and look defensive, use a more open stance with your body. This is a sign of confidence and helps you feel more social.
- **Smile.** A confident person smiles more often.

BODY LANGUAGE & BULLIES

Bullies look for reactions such as your:
- Facial expressions
- Body language
- Tone of voice.

Communication skills to learn to deal with bullies:
- Use eye contact
- Speak with a clear voice
- Stand up straight
- Have a friendly look on your face
- Have a positive answer when speaking to the bully.

To practise these skills, stand in front of a mirror and pretend the bully is in front of you, or video yourself and play it back.

THE POWER OF WORDS

Japanese scientist, Dr. Masaru Emoto revolutionised the idea our thoughts and intentions impact the physical world around us. His water experiments involved exposing bottles of water to various words, pictures or music, then freezing the water and examining the frozen crystals under a microscope.

Dr Emoto's work is documented in the book *Messages from Water*[1], and shows water exposed to positive intentions (words, thoughts) resulted in beautiful complete crystals, while negative intentions resulted in malformed and misshapen crystal formations.

His work helps us realise that if water is affected by words and intentions, what about human beings, who are made of mostly

---

1   Emoto, Masaru. 1943-2014. *The Hidden Messages in Water*. Hillsboro, Or. : [Emeryville, CA] :Beyond Words Pub. ; Distributed to the trade by Publishers Group West, 2004.

water? Our thoughts and words not only affect ourselves, but the world around us.

> ★ Watch Angie's video for this experiment in the interactive book. You can also see photos of the water crystals exposed to words, music, photographs and prayers at deanpublishing.com/angieclucas ★

The rice experiment was invented by Dr Masaru Emoto as an alternative to his water experiment. The goal of the experiment is to show that a person's attitude towards anything, even rice, affects what happens to it.

Create your own rice experiment:

1. Gather 3 glass jars without labels. Ensure all jars are clean and the same size/shape.
2. Cook 1 cup of rice and split it between 3 jars and place the lids on.
3. Label 1 x jar 'Love', 1 x jar 'Hate' and leave 1 x jar unlabelled (or whatever words work for you 'Gratitude', 'Thankful', 'You're Amazing', 'Worthless', 'Failure', etc.)
4. Place all jars in the same location with the same amount of light and temperature.
5. Each day for 30 days:
   » Say words and think thoughts of gratitude to the 'Love' jar i.e. thank you, I love you, you're amazing, etc.
   » Say words and think thoughts of negativity to the 'Hate' jar i.e. you're an idiot, I hate you, etc.
   » Ignore the unlabelled jar.
6. At the end of the 30 days, notice the difference between the jars. If rice is affected by our thoughts and words…imagine what the person our words are aimed at feels!

"Words are free. It's how you use them,
that may cost you."

Unknown Author

Chapter 3

CREATING MOMENTUM

"Imagination is more important than knowledge."

Albert Einstein

IMAGINATION IS POWERFUL

I remember a moment in time when I was in my first year at high school, sitting on a bench seat at lunchtime in the school grounds. I never looked forward to lunchtime, unlike the other kids. This was actually the worst part of the day for me as this was when I was most exposed to the bullies. At lunchtime there were no teachers around, plus I had to deal with all of the students at school, not just the ones in my class because at lunchtime everyone was outside in the grounds at the same time.

Most kids would wait with excitement when it was time for the school bell to ring for lunch. Not me — instead, I would start bracing myself and go into protection mode, waiting for the sound of that dreaded bell. I felt I was the only one.

On this particular day, I was feeling more alone than usual. Even though there were other kids around me, no one was engaging with me or including me in anything. I was having a really down day. This actually didn't happen to me as often as it had in the past, now that I was older, but today was just one of those days. All the little issues were starting to stack up and get to me again, and I started slipping into that familiar cycle of thinking, "life just isn't fair". When I had these days, everything seemed to become a problem even when nothing had really changed. The only difference was that I was letting my head fill up with negative thoughts.

As I sat on the school bench seat every lunchtime, most days kids would walk past me and start laughing because my feet couldn't reach the ground. This was an issue I dealt with every day but today, for no apparent reason other than how I was feeling, it had become a major problem. I started feeling really uncomfortable. I couldn't reach the ground like all the other kids, and I was over them teasing me every time they walked past, just because my feet were hanging in the air instead of resting on the concrete underneath, like everyone else.

> "Imagination is everything. It is the preview of life's coming attractions."
>
> **Albert Einstein**

In the next minute or two, I just sat there trying to process what I was feeling. Then, in a split-second before my mind had time to catch up, for some reason I started moving my legs around in circles. I'd started doing this subconsciously but then realised why I'd started doing it — it was to change the way I was feeling — I was doing something different to snap out of my negative thoughts — I wanted to get on with my day! And this negativity was getting me nowhere! So, I 'swung' into action.

Then, just as I was sitting there swinging circles with my feet, an amazing thing happened. To my sheer surprise, some other kids started copying me and doing the same thing! And then it spread like a fad; nearly all the kids were doing it — even the ones that had been laughing at me before stopped and now joined in! They tried to make the same circles as me. Some found it easy, but some were finding it a bit of a challenge because their legs were just too long!

This made me feel great as I had something unique that others were interested in and wanted to copy. The thing I'd started had caught on and this created an opportunity for me to share it with them, and to show them how to do it. Suddenly, they were engaging with me as a 'normal' human being which gave me a sense of belonging. And even if it was just in the moment, it felt really good. I was now not the joke to walk past and laugh at, but the person who swung her legs in circles and this was a 'cool' thing to do. This changed how the others saw me from then on.

CHANGING YOUR MINDSET

When I found my inner courage that day at school, I decided to start making some changes in my life. I now understood, that for me to be able to take control of which direction my life would be lived, it was up to no one else, but me.

Swinging my legs was a positive action, and the reaction I got felt good. It gave me a confidence boost. Finally, the other kids started respecting me and communicating with me on an equal level.

This is just one small example of my experience in changing my mindset to overcome negative thinking. Just by changing my attitude at that moment, within a few seconds the environment around me started changing too because it had a spin-off effect: Instead of sitting in my usual position on that one bench seat in the playground, I did something new, positive and different, and others noticed.

LIFE'S WHAT YOU MAKE IT

The choice is yours. No matter how much others rally around you with support, they cannot be of any help to you unless you have the courage to step up to the plate yourself. You must decide that now is the time to put 100 per cent into you to be ready to start a new way of life. Having the courage to take total control of every decision you need to make and each direction you want to take, will set you up for a much more enjoyable life.

You, and no one but you, can make the best out of your life. It only takes courage and small positive steps to create momentum to move forward to having a better life. Decide you can, and once you make this very important decision you will see changes in the way you think. You will have less negative thinking and more positive thoughts.

MOVING FORWARD

Be true to yourself and others. When you learn to become honest with yourself, you can bring out your pure soul. This is the start to living from the heart within you — the point in your life when everything will start changing — when you finally unhide your true character from behind your own barriers. These are the walls that you have put up over your lifetime to protect you from the outside world.

You will start to see that you have a very strong inner self. You will start to realise and be surprised at the inner strength of your character, and at how much resilience you have in the big scary world that we live in today.

When you can start accepting who you really are, then you can be happy in identifying your strengths and weaknesses. Once you find within yourself, clarity about who is your real self, then you can progress and take on any issues that have been holding you back in life.

Moving forward, you can start looking at things like, for example, how you manage uncertainty. You take responsibility for your own thoughts and behaviours and this really helps when you find yourself in tough situations. The person that understands you the most is you. It's true for all of us and we need to manage our emotions to help put our issues in perspective.

These skills help us to respond to events and issues with much more certainty which in turn gives us the ability to take ownership of the results of our choices, and to create the pathways that we wish for our lives. When you can be present with yourself, you can maintain a greater level of calmness and this helps in making better decisions.

We all need to be aware that it takes time for us to make these kinds of changes, but we can do so by taking small steps over time. Working on becoming the best version of yourself will lead you down a new path to having a much improved life — something most of us want and look for.

With all of that, always remember to take time out to have fun. You need to be able to take things lightly sometimes.

Enjoy life while you're on your life journey.

STANDING TALL FROM THE INSIDE

List 5 of your inner strengths (i.e. patience, kindness, resilience, positivity, caring, determination, a good listener, courage).

....

....

....

....

....

List 5 of your other strengths (outer) — things you are good at, skills that you have.

....

....

....

....

....

List 5 areas you'd like to improve and build into strengths (you class as a weakness) i.e. disorganised, self-critical, trouble saying no to friends.

....

....

....

....

....

....

....

What action can you take to change and strengthen the areas you see as weaknesses?

....

....

....

....

....

....

....

....

....

....

....

ONLY FOCUS ON WHAT YOU CAN CONTROL

What you say to yourself is more important than what anyone else says to you. Supportive self-talk is the very important foundation of creating a peaceful state-of-mind. When you learn the skill of building positive self-esteem, you learn the key to developing powerful self-confidence.

You need to understand that whenever you are in contact with someone there will be a feeling created in each person; either good or bad, depending on how they are treated. By being mindful of this, you can then become more aware of how you communicate with others. The world will always become a better place if we are all playing our part in treating each other respectfully.

Your thoughts trigger both your conscious and your subconscious mind to decide what you focus on. Every time the emotion of worry, for example, arises it strengthens the neural pathways in your brain to focus on worrying. To be able to reprogram your brain to help you refocus on what you want, use the power of positive thoughts. These are essential in achieving the best results and creating the best pathways for your life.

Having a look at what you are able to control in your life (versus what is out of your control) can help you focus correctly and not waste time on stuff that is not fixable by you. You must then take actions on only what you can do something about and trash the things that will drain you and give no results.

Sometimes it can be helpful to make a list of what you can control and what you can't control. That way, you can understand what to focus on more clearly.

WHAT I CAN'T CONTROL

~~Other people's moods~~

WHAT I CAN CONTROL

How I respond to others ✓

"Focus on your future, you can
never reverse the past."
Angie Clucas

I practice spending my time on positive things and am always trying to improve my environment, such as people I choose to be around me. I do what is possible for me to make improvements, or at least find the right person to help me fix something if I don't have the skills to do so myself. There is always a way to improve. It's just a matter of you making the vision and then the decision, to do so.

It's time to get rid of the Itty Bitty Shitty Committee! Pay attention to your self-talk. Negative self-talk may be a fleeting thought (a small criticism of yourself) or you may dwell on it for days. It's about catching yourself in the moment and changing the negative self-talk to positive i.e. 'I can't believe I was so stupid' to 'This took courage and I am proud of myself for giving it a go, 'I can't do this' to 'If I get out of my own way, what else is possible?' and 'I'm such a failure' to 'Even though it wasn't the outcome I hoped for, I learned a lot about myself'.

It can be helpful to make a list so you can remember what to say and what not to say to yourself.

THINGS TO STOP SAYING   THINGS TO START SAYING

I'm so stupid   I am smart ✓

FINDING INSPIRATION

Just like I used Einstein's quotes to inspire me, you can use inspirational quotes to change your mindset. What quote have you seen whose words inspired you? Add these quotes on your wall or mirror, or as your screensaver on your phone or computer. How do you find them? Insta, Pinterest or Google the name of someone you find inspiring i.e. 'Albert Einstein quotes' and see what shows up. Switch the search results view to images and you'll find quotes ready to download/print. You can even type in 'inspirational quotes' and see what comes up.

> ★ You can view an example of quotes you may find online in the interactive book at deanpublishing.com/angieclucas ★

> *"I never try to impress anyone.*
> *I'm just happy to be me."*
> **Angie Clucas**

Chapter 4

FINDING YOUR REAL DEAL

"Knowing yourself is the beginning of all wisdom."

Aristotle

CREATE VALUE

The day that I started high school was scary and exciting all at the same time, and a bit confronting: High school brought together all the kids from a large number of primary schools in the area and rolled us into one. For some kids like me who came from a small school in a country town, this was especially daunting. Suddenly, we were exposed to a large number of new people in a much bigger school environment and had to adapt in a short amount of time.

Because we were now part of this new combined group of school kids, our old primary school class immediately ceased to exist. We were put into brand new classes mixed in with the other kids. So, the group of kids I knew from primary school who were my friends, was now split up, and I was surrounded by unfamiliar faces. I knew this was the same for everyone as we were all new to high school, but for me being in this situation always presented an extra challenge, as people would pick me out.

I scanned my surroundings, however, there was no time to deal with this yet as the next challenge came straight away. We had to quickly choose the subjects we wanted to do which also determined who you'd be in class with for each subject. But at this stage, we didn't know each other and so we couldn't choose classes that would be with our friends. I think at this point we were all a bit shocked, as this was a much different school life than what we were used to. For the first time, we were making decisions about which direction our lives were going which even in this small way, seemed pretty big.

So, the day went on and we were all just doing what we had to do, including the kids I'd turned up with from our primary school. Then, one of the girls from another school said, "hello" to me, and just because of this we started talking. Later we sat and ate our lunch together. This was a new experience for me, people I didn't know never came up to me and asked me questions about my day. This girl seemed to be genuinely interested in me as a person. She was not making fun of me.

Julie and I became good friends at high school, and to this day over 30 years on in 2020, we are still great friends.

One day, many years later, Julie explained to me that after that first day when we met, she went home and asked her mum for advice: She asked her what she should 'do' as she'd met this person that seemed nice but was short and a little different. Julie's Mum told her, "just treat her like anyone else and see what happens".

I will always be forever grateful for that great advice. It's advice that I myself try to practise every day because I know that it can make such a difference to someone's day. It could even mean, like it did for Julie and me, the start of a new friendship that could last a lifetime.

STANDING TALL FROM THE INSIDE

When you make the effort to put yourself forward so that someone new can meet you — even if you don't feel confident or strong — this shows strength and is a brave action. It shows people that you're open to the idea of making friends, standing in your own skin as you are, being real and friendly.

This in itself often brings rewards: Even if the person you meet that day doesn't end up becoming a friend, the experiences you gather when you practise being open to meeting new people helps you progress. Experiencing different and new reactions, both good and bad from the people you meet, helps you learn how to not be afraid and to become more confident. It helps you become better at choosing and making friends.

Never underestimate the impact you have on other people. Find your 'real deal' within you.

GOOD INFLUENCES VERSUS BAD INFLUENCES

A good question to ask yourself: Who is a good influence for me, who is not a good influence for me? It can sometimes be hard to know at first but it's important to discern the difference.

Bad Influences: try to make you do things you don't want to do, or try to influence you to act or behave a certain way. They can try to dominate you and not let you make any decisions. They usually always try to coerce you to their way of thinking or acting. Some bad influences ask you to lie or not tell the entire truth about something. If someone if trying to influence the way you

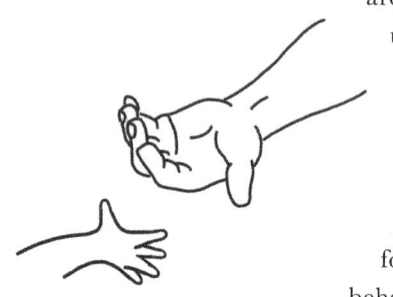

are naturally or forcing you into an uncomfortable position – they are a bad influence.

Good Influences: let you be yourself and like you for who you are. They don't use force to get their way or make you behave a certain way. They respect you and encourage you toward your goals and dreams. They are happy for you and treat you well. They never coerce you into uncomfortable situations and always respect your decisions.

HELPING SOMEONE 'DIFFERENT'

Helping someone 'different' is the same as helping anyone else, and these points apply to everyone:

- Everyone deserves to be treated with respect.
- Everyone has a choice about how they act, and how they act is their responsibility.
- Everyone has a right to feel safe in this world and to feel that they belong.

List any times where you stepped out of your comfort zone (and your circle of friends) to reach out and help someone who was different.

....

....

....

....

....

....

....

....

....

....

....

....

What did it feel like to help?

....

....

....

....

....

....

....

....

....

....

....

....

....

List 3 occasions in the future where you could help someone and how.

....

....

....

....

....

....

....

....

....

....

....

....

THE GOOD, THE BAD, AND THE BETTER

You must remind yourself that when you get a bad reaction from someone that you're being friendly towards, even if they are mean or nasty towards you, don't let it bring you down. Stand tall and remind yourself of who you are. You're the one being friendly, and that's good, not bad.

Remind yourself that they are just not aware that their skills in behaviour need to improve. They're probably just reacting to you that way because they don't know any different. It doesn't make their behaviour right. But if you can deal with it this way, it gives you a chance to make the situation better, instead of getting cut up by their knee-jerk reaction. This helps you move on in a positive way. An added benefit is that often this rubs off on the other person, as they see you being not just friendly but strong, and you can't beat that.

> *"I know that I belong in this world and I will always try to add value to someone's day."*
>
> **Angie Clucas**

FIRST IMPRESSIONS ALWAYS COUNT

The first few 'words' of your body language when you meet a new person is something that you can't take back and usually, that person will remember this when dealing with you in the future. It's human nature and we all do it, but usually the choice is yours as to how you act when you meet someone. This will affect their first impression of you, and vice-versa.

That day, when I learnt what Julie's Mum had said, it rang so true — you only get one chance to make a first impression on someone. I have always remembered this when I meet new people, I will always hold my head up high and give the impression that I am happy to live within my own skin. I know that I belong in this world and I will always try to add value to someone's day even if we don't speak or smile or even wave to each other. It costs nothing but gives a lot: it's a gift that you can give a stranger or a friend for free so "why not" I say.

How do you smile at someone when you first meet them i.e. do you give them your full attention, do you smile with your eyes also?

....

....

....

....

....

....

....

How do you feel when you meet new people i.e. happy, excited, nervous, shy, distracted?

....

....

....

....

....

....

....

....

....

What are some ways you can help yourself and people you first meet, feel comfortable?

....

....

....

....

....

....

....

....

Can you think of a time when you made a good first impression? What did you say or do?

....

....

....

....

....

....

....

....

Angie is sharing more in her INTERACTIVE book.

See exclusive, behind-the-scenes videos, audios and photos.

DOWNLOAD free content and learn how to live your best life.

deanpublishing.com/angieclucas

Chapter 5

I SMELL TROUBLE

"Remember that children pick their role models from adults closest to them."

Angie Clucas

KNOWLEDGE COMES FROM EXPERIENCE

> "Information is not knowledge. The only
> source of knowledge is experience."
>
> Albert Einstein

When I was 13 years old, my class went on a school excursion to the city. I lived in a country town, so this was an adventure. We were given a task: The teacher was trying to get us to do some sort of survey in a suburb of Christchurch that the school had chosen for us. We had to learn a set of questions that the teacher had put together for us, and then we were to go door knocking in the area to ask people the questions.

The night before we were to undertake this activity, I couldn't sleep as this idea just didn't sit well with me. I mentioned my concerns to a couple of other students but no one else seemed to have any issues about what the teacher was asking us to do.

The closer the bus got to our destination, the more my tummy was turning itself inside-out. Every bone in my body was aching as my intuition was telling me that this situation was wrong. It went against every rule that my parents had taught me, and I couldn't believe that a school was about to put us into danger. And nobody except me, seemed to be rattled by it or even care.

The experiences that I'd suffered in the past had now in this specific moment, helped me decide that I wasn't going to go into some strangers' yard and knock on their front door, not knowing what was on the other side of that door and that it potentially could be dangerous. In my head I was thinking, *what happened to 'stranger danger'?* This once national campaign slogan was not now as common in 1980 but the message was still very clear in my mind.

Once the teacher called out my name, I decided it was "now or never". I had to speak up! Even if every part of my body was shaking, I knew I must tell the teacher that I was refusing to take part in this activity! I managed to get my words out, but the teacher just brushed me off, grabbed hold of my hand and told me to "stop being silly". This made me feel sick to my stomach. *This teacher is being a bully,* I thought. To me, the actions of this teacher were no better than the bullies I'd encountered in the school yard.

I was already going to be in trouble, so I closed my eyes and spoke to my inner self, *You are not being respected by this teacher. He is not listening to what I thought was a reasonable request.* So, once the teacher had stopped pairing everyone up, I once again voiced my concerns. The teacher told me to "go and sit on the bus". He said, "I'll deal with you later".

In the meantime, as it turned out, by me standing up to the teacher and voicing my concerns, other students then started realising that maybe I had a point. It made them start to get a bit nervous about the activity too. But my understanding of the situation was different because I had experienced these feelings many times before when being bullied. Because of this, I was able to assess this type of problem very quickly and react using my inner sensor alarm.

By the time the other students returned to the bus, they were all talking about how scary that activity really was. They said I was the only one that sensed how dangerous it could have been; that they'd never before even thought about the environments they'd just been entering: strangers' yards where they had no idea what could have happened to them.

Yes, I got into trouble and had to write out some lines for not doing as the teacher requested. But those students learnt a big lesson that day about being mindful of your environment at all times. No matter who tells you it's okay to enter into unfamiliar situations, listen to your inner alarm! And, act on it! It worked for me that day — even though every part of my body and voice was shaking standing up to the teacher — only because I was strong enough to voice my fears.

"You must always listen to your inner detector to help you navigate life."

Angie Clucas

THE DAMAGE DONE BY BULLYING

Bullying causes so much damage, in so many ways. The effects can be physical, mental and emotional and usually go together. Some damage is easier to see because the signs are visible, for example:

- cuts, scratches and bruises
- headaches, backaches and stomach aches
- skin problems as a result of a nervous condition
- sleeping difficulties and nightmares
- eating disorders
- habitual poor posture
- physical self-harm
- anxiety, depression.

SIGNS RUN DEEP

And sometimes, the signs are harder to see but just as real, for example:

- lack of concentration
- learning difficulties
- lack of motivation
- avoiding extra school activities
- over-sensitivity and fear of receiving feedback from anyone
- kids deliberately not doing their best so that they intentionally get 'left out': Sometimes kids, especially ones who usually do well at school, do this as a way to get someone to notice that something's wrong.

GET OUT OF THE BULLY'S BUBBLE

If you're in real trouble as a consequence of being bullied and feel like you're trapped in a bubble, tell someone you feel can help with it. Getting help is the right thing to do.

DEALING WITH FEELINGS

We all have lot of feelings, sometimes we feel angry, happy, sad, indifferent, jealous, curious and lot lots more. Being human means that we have feelings. I have had my fair share of feeling worthless and not good enough, but I also figured out that these feelings weren't helping me feel better — they were making me feel worse. But I discovered that building my strength and character helped me get stronger inside and learning how to boost myself when times were tough was crucial to overcoming adversity.

When you are going through some tough times, it is easy to start to doubt yourself. When we are young, we live in our own little playful worlds where we believe anything is possible. As children we do not have any understanding about the adult world and it never seems to be important to us except when we get told off or we hurt ourselves. Children live in their own rational world that is protected by superheroes and our family support group of adults.

Once we get a little older and we start to take more accountability for our actions, this is when life lessons start to come our way whether we are ready to take them on or not. It's part of growing up, but it's not always easy. When I first learnt that life was different outside my little bubble, I realised that some people could be cruel and sometimes life was unfair. It wasn't easy to accept. But I slowly began to build myself up and learn how to become more resilient. I did this so life didn't push me around.

When we believe that we can do anything we put our minds to then we don't let the big wide world swallow us up and spit us out. But sometimes life puts us through the wringer and tests us in every conceivable way. These events are part of the journey of life. If you are living your life to the fullest then the more effort you put into everything, the more you experience life. Sometimes it's good and sometimes it's not.

When issues arise in our lives, we need to take them on and not let them fester. The worst thing that you can do is let some issues consume you because this is how they start to control your life. It's the same way bullies do…they start to control people's lives too.

The best way thing you can do is be your own superhero. Stay in control of your issues both big and small. I know that this is not always easy but if we can learn the skills to be able to deal with events and troubles early, then issues don't take over our space for any length of time. We must learn to become experts of resilience. We must learn to let go of the small stuff that doesn't matter but face the stuff that does matter head-on.

Sorting out what is valuable to you personally and what you need to leave behind will put you in a better place.

To make this work, it can help to think of your brain as a computer program. A program that can be changed. Like a new type of software. It's time to put all the old stuff you thought held you back and controlled your life into the trash. All that negative stuff. So, everything that makes you feel bad about yourself or makes a bully happy…TRASH IT! You can even close your eyes and practise dumping stuff — imagine that it's like a virus and you need to dump it to clear your software. This will give you a fresh start with a new computer program in your brain. Now there's room to replace it with a new program.

Your new thoughts will help you:
- have a positive attitude about yourself
- have strong eye contact with others
- look confident
- speak with a clear voice
- occupy the space you hold.

A more confident program will also help when confronting a bully. In this program, you are an individual who deserves to be treated with respect, and you must treat everyone the way you wish to be treated yourself, including the bully! Otherwise, it doesn't work. If you go back to being negative and powerless, it just feeds the bully and the bully gets worse. And if you start bullying the bully, you become a bully yourself. So, stop the cycle! Break the cycle by empowering yourself and calling the bullying out.

You can 'switch on' your new program today! TRASH the spam that's been occupying your brain and run a new program.

What are 3 thoughts or things you can do to switch ON your new attitude?

....

....

....

....

....

....

....

....

....

....

....

....

....

USING POSITIVE TACTICS

You have to prepare an answer for the bully when they are teasing you so that you take the power away from them and give it back to yourself, where it belongs. For example, when kids used to tease me and say, "Why are you so short?" I would tell them, "This is what happens when you don't eat your vegies". That surprised them as they weren't expecting me to be funny, positive or confident. They didn't know what to do. They didn't know how to react.

Using positive tactics to deal with bullies means not just on the bully, but also on yourself. For example, if you're not feeling strong one day and you know that where you're going, you'll need to deal with a bully, change your environment if you can; go somewhere else that day from where you normally go, like the library at lunchtime instead of the playground. Just somewhere to have a break to get your strength back. It's smart to be nice to yourself.

REGULATING YOUR FEELINGS

In bad situations, some people get sad; some get mad. Whatever the case is for you, these reactions come from your feelings and are part of your survival instinct; your inbuilt mechanism to survive against danger. When your brain identifies a threat to your safety, it sends a message to your pituitary and adrenal glands requesting energy to act. Your 'survival' hormones are released which enable you to fight or run (known as 'fight-or-flight'). These hormones influence everything we do like running, eating and breathing as well as everything we feel and experience. So, when a person's mind and emotions are overtaken by stress, like they can be when you're being bullied, their body reacts: the adrenalin and hormones kick in and this can cause the body to go into overload.

Unless you can release your feelings, you may become powerless or paralysed because when you bottle up your feelings, they get stuck inside, until they just have to burst out.

Regardless of whether you ignore your feelings or not, challenging the bully with aggression isn't a great idea, it only spurs them on and makes you more vulnerable. Once you can regulate (adjust) your painful feelings such as anger or fear, you will be able to think more clearly. Thinking clearly will help you develop a much more sensible plan to deal with the bully. This approach will make you much more relaxed, and also less likely to give the bully their expected satisfaction. This is why managing your own feelings first, helps you to make the correct decisions for yourself, and can help you control your actions when confronted by a bully.

3-POINT CHECKLIST TO REGULATE YOUR EMOTIONS

Here is an on-the-spot 'feeling' checklist to use, when you need to regulate your emotions:

1. What
Identify what you are feeling. Is it anger? Is it sadness? Loneliness? Maybe all of the above, or something else.

2. How much
Put a quantity on it. How much are you feeling the feelings? How much are they affecting you? Are you feeling mostly comfortable or uncomfortable? Okay or not okay? Really.

3. Release
Work out how to release the feelings that are making you feel uncomfortable. Some on-the-spot quick ways you can do this are to:

- count to ten
- take some deep breaths
- think of something fun
- play sport
- change your environment
- talk to a friend.

Even doing one of these things can give you enough time to regulate your feelings. And if you're being bullied, this is very helpful because you'll feel stronger quickly, and then be able to deal with the bully better.

Learning how to regulate your feelings is a life skill you can use every day. You can use it forever, not only when you quickly need to deal with a bully.

There are loads of ways to do this — it depends on how you're feeling. Here are some examples:

RELEASING YOUR ANGER

- Do some exercise, e.g. go for a walk or a run, or use a punching bag.
- Blow up some balloons (sounds silly but it can work!).
- Write your feelings down. This is a very effective tool you can do almost anywhere.
- Go somewhere quiet to cool down.

There are literally hundreds of things you can do. The main thing is to do one.

What are 3 things you can do to release your anger?

....

....

....

....

....

....

....

....

....

DEALING WITH SADNESS

Rather than stopping yourself from crying, sometimes it's better to just let it out. It's an emotional release from our body that helps us move forward, like releasing anger, dealing with sadness starts by releasing it. Here are some ways to help:

- Help yourself to release some tears by for example:
  » peeling an onion
  » watching a sad movie.

- Take time out to just be sad (that's okay). You could for example:
  » burn a candle
  » go somewhere peaceful.

What are 3 things you can do release sadness?

....

....

....

....

....

....

....

....

....

....

Choose to be sad for 10 minutes. At 10 minutes, ask yourself if you'd like to remain sad? Or is this no longer working for you and you'd like to choose something different? There is no right or wrong, it's recognising that it's just a choice to remain in the space you're in or choose something that aligns with where you'd like to be.

DEALING WITH STRESS

Doing things on a regular basis to relieve stress is good and can be fun. There are heaps of things you can do, but here are a few simple ones:

- Have a bath or a shower
- Blow some bubbles
- Walk up and down stairs
- Do a hobby you enjoy
- Spend time with your pet
- Play a physical game — go for a run, have a kick of the footy, play basketball
- Talk to someone
- Spend time colouring in or drawing
- Watch a funny movie
- Call a help line simply to have a chat about your feelings
- Listen to a relaxing meditation on YouTube
- Book in with a counsellor and ask them for ideas on dealing with stress.

In situations where you feel stress, what can
you do to feel calmer?

....

....

....

....

....

....

....

List 3 ways you can centre your body, be present and calm when
you are stuck, angry, fearful. i.e. Count to 3, take 3-5 deep breaths
into your belly, feel your feet, think of something positive, count
backwards from 10, write your feelings in a journal, etc.

....

....

....

....

....

....

....

....

....

....

....

"Try. Otherwise you will never know
what you are capable of."

Angie Clucas

Chapter 6

GOING TO ARNHEM LAND

"Your thoughts affect your moods.
Smiles are contagious.
Kindness is free."

Angie Clucas

FOLLOW YOUR
CURIOSITY

> "I have no special talent. I am only
> passionately curious."
>
> **Albert Einstein**

It had been three years since I'd left high school and I'd been working at the local bakery in Darfield since then. It was my very first workplace job and I'd worked there with no issues. I was quite happy there, growing as a person and collecting new skills along the way. My life seemed to be going along just fine until something totally unexpected happened — and as a

19-year-old, I had no idea what impact this was going to have on my life.

Leading up to this event were a combination of things that took place over a period of six months, starting on the day that my boss said he was "going to put the business on the market". I didn't really know how this would change things; it was my first job. So, I was just working, but 'business as usual' was to about to be no more.

The day the business was sold, and I got a new boss, was the day that my world in Darfield started falling apart. He started to change things around; he employed a new staff member who happened to be a neighbour of mine. We knew each other well because we'd grown up and gone to school together for most of our school lives. So, at first, I thought, *Well, this is okay.*

How wrong was I!

First, my hours started getting cut. Next, the other person was taking over my work. I asked my new boss why this was happening. He came straight back at me with this answer: "You are too short for this job."

I said to him, "So, I haven't done anything wrong while I've been working here." He replied, "No, I have no issue with you except — you're not tall enough for the work that's required." Well, this sounded wrong as I'd been working there for three years with no problems at all. Not only that, my old boss had given me a fantastic reference when he left and sold the business. (We actually stayed in touch for many years thereafter as friends.) What was this new boss's problem? I was then told that my hours would go down from five days-a-week to two!

I was shocked. This just wasn't right. I didn't deserve this. Why was this happening? It really knocked my self-esteem around. There was no real reason for this treatment. Being short was not a reason. It was something he was using against me to push me out. And he thought this was okay because he was the boss.

BULLY BOSSES

A bully who is also a boss can be tricky to deal with. He or she may think that having authority over you in a workplace means that they can bully you. They may think that's okay. But it isn't. It's wrong.

They may try to make you think that you need them, so that they can push you around. Trust your instincts if you feel this is happening. Find a better option. And make your exit quick.

No one needs a controlling bully in their life.

Things were not good at the bakery anymore and I couldn't do just two days-a-week. That wasn't enough. I needed another option. So, there was nothing else to do but find some more work. But I had to do this while still dealing with this bully of a boss who seemed intent on wearing me down.

Pretty soon, I managed to get some causal work at the local fruit and vegie shop, but this was just a short-term solution. I really wanted a full-time job, in a workplace where my skills would be valued. I needed a change.

I thought about it and looked at my options. There didn't seem much in Darfield as it was only a small town and I didn't have another job to jump to anywhere else. Then, I remembered an offer my godparents had made me: Kath, my godmother had said if I wanted to, I could come up to Arnhem Land in the Northern Territory of Australia. A place called Oenpelli. I hadn't really considered it before, but now it looked like a really good option. I decided to go!

Once I made the decision to move, I went and got a job picking garlic to pay for my ticket. It would take a number of months before I would have enough money saved up, but eventually I got there. I bought an open return ticket for 12 months, so that at any point if it didn't work out, I could go back home. I left my options open. I had nothing to lose. And even though I was terrified at the prospect of this huge lifestyle change, I knew within myself that I needed it — I needed to try.

I understood that changing my environment and moving to another country meant that I would be leaving home. I'd lived in New Zealand all my life so far, so this was something completely new. I was going somewhere where no one (not even my godparents really) knew me or my past. I knew this would grow my character to become a stronger person. I would have to provide for myself — and stand on my own two feet without the safety net of my family and friends — to create a life that I could eventually look back on and be proud of in my dying days. Deep down inside, I had a desire to prove to myself that I was not that 'little girl' that most people (with the exception of my family) saw me as.

I packed up all my gear into one suitcase and got ready for my adventure into the unknown! Then, on the 7th March 1990 after saying a very sad goodbye to my family, I boarded my plane to Arnhem Land.

It was hard saying goodbye, but I knew deep down that this was the right thing for  me to do. I needed to go on this journey to find out who I really was. I couldn't believe that I'd actually achieved the first step so far, and this quest I'd started about six months back was now becoming very real. To my amazement, I was not stressed at all. I actually felt that I would be able to handle it. I also knew that I could go home at any time if I had to, so this was a choice.

When I left Christchurch airport it was 1°C outside with frost on the ground and the sun was just starting to appear in the sky.

I only took one suitcase because that's all that I could handle. I travelled with a small backpack on the plane, the size that most kids take to school so I could put it under the seat in front of me and use it as a foot rest because my feet couldn't reach the floor. Because I'm not tall enough to reach the overhead lockers, I made sure that I avoided that situation by carrying my small backpack. I didn't want to hold up the passengers desperate to get off while I waited for the flight attendant to help me.

Almost ten hours later, we arrived at Darwin Airport and it was 30°C outside. I wasn't used to this type of heat coming from New Zealand and still had all my 'NZ' clothes on of course.

Back in 1990, the 'old' Darwin airport as we call it now, was a very basic airport, as I was about to find out. We walked from the plane down the 'air stairs' and across the tarmac to what I thought was the workshop hanger. To my amazement, it was actually the bag collection area. I thought with curiosity and a little bit of amusement, *So, this is Darwin's Airport. No air conditioning here, just overhead fans.* It was simple. It didn't bother me at all, it was just a new experience, a surprise. My first impression of Darwin. A 'no frills' place.

Soon after, I was met by one of Kath's friends as Kath couldn't get into town until the next day. I was really feeling the heat now and couldn't get off my layers of clothes fast enough! We collected my one and only suitcase and got in the car for the drive to Oenpelli.

By the time we got there, it was already dark. So, I had to wait until the next day to see what the place was like. For now, it was time to turn in for the night. I tried to get to sleep, but it was really hard that first night. I remember it well because I didn't get any sleep: There was a fan over my head in bed, and I kept thinking it would fall on top of me — which it didn't of course — but I thought it was going to and instead of sleeping, I stayed awake all night thinking about my new life, *This is going to take some getting used to!*

Well, the next morning I got my next big shock as I discovered Oenpelli on the outside. Everything had a layer of red dirt over it! All the roads were dirt roads, and pretty much all of them covered in bull dust which seemed to get into everything. Bull dust is an ultra-fine red dust which kicks up into a dust cloud when you drive through it. It can be very hazardous to vehicles and livestock and they can get bogged in it. This fine red dust (which got its name in the 1920s, apparently because it resembles the soil trampled by cattle in stockyards) is a distinctive feature of the Australian outback.

My first week in Oenpelli was a very big learning curve. There was no time to waste. Straight away, I had to stand up by myself and take control of my life. This is exactly what I'd come for, but I guess I didn't realise how different it would be here, compared to the life I'd known. I told myself, I'd just have to adjust quickly because there were things that I had to get on to immediately.

To start with, I had to find some work and at the same time get used to working in these conditions which was so removed from where I'd come from. I also had to get myself an Aussie driver's licence which turned out to be another experience. I had Kath's car to practice in and the first time I drove it, all the kids in the area came out and lined the road, clapping at me driving up the dirt road for the first time. This was such a weird experience that I didn't know how to react. I just thought, "Well, I guess all I can do is go along with them." I even used the horn a couple of times which they seemed to love, I figured at least I was making their day.

I guess my driving practice must have been entertaining because these noisy kids just kept on following me! When I arrived at the police station to sit my driving test, the policeman came outside to see what all the commotion was about. I just put my hands up in the air and said, "I have no idea what all this is about." The policeman just laughed and said, "You had better come inside."

I passed the test and got my licence. After that, over time the novelty of me driving around the area must have started waning as the lines of clapping noisy kids on the road started dropping off.

That special day, for the first time in a long time, I felt like I was starting to regain some control over my life again. I felt the energy to deal with whatever life was going to hit me with from then on — I had a new sense of being able to move forward, and to live my life in a direction that I could be happy in taking.

One day, I asked one of the local men why the kids had been cheering and clapping when I drove the car. He told me that they couldn't work out how someone the same size as a kid was able to drive a car.

This event was the start of me becoming accepted into the community. I was able to just be me and be comfortable in my own skin, without having the pressure of trying to prove myself. I was just being myself and everyone within this community was generally happy for me to belong. I was really starting to find my confidence — my true self. This was the change I was looking for: I could start building my life, growing my character, and becoming independent in a relaxed environment where I felt safe and comfortable, and part of the community.

After being in Oenpelli for a couple of weeks I got some part-time work in the school as a teacher's aide, something that I would never have done back in NZ because of the experiences I had in my own school life. This was now the 'new me' taking up new challenges. Getting out of my own way. I was getting on with my life and not letting my self-doubt stop me from growing into the new better version of myself I'd been looking for. I could be proud and respected as a member of the community.

I'd landed in this new place, got a good job and was fitting in well. Things were looking good. And even though I was still a bit nervous because everything was new, it was really exciting!

Once I got started at the school and my nerves settled down, I started to enjoy this new role as a teacher's aide. These kids needed a lot of help learning to read and write because as indigenous Australians, English was not their main language. As I saw the kids improve and grow, I got great satisfaction — we grew together, learning new skills, and shared pride in our achievements. We learnt about each other's values and what was important to us as a group and as individuals.

So, life went on in Oenpelli. I continued working on myself and growing, learning and settling into my new community and home.

Later, I went on to work at the local supermarket and started servicing outstations by plane. This was another great experience as I learnt a lot about the indigenous people that live in the remote bush lands of Australia. These people hadn't been affected by alcohol (a problem affecting some towns and communities). They still went hunting and gathering as they had for thousands of years. Spending time with these people showed me that you can choose to lead a simple life and be happy and content. It doesn't have to be complicated. Sometimes 'simple' is best.

GIVING YOURSELF A CHANCE

Sometimes you land on your feet and grow as a person from experiencing things that you couldn't have dreamed of happening before. By taking that huge leap of faith and moving to another place and having the courage to step way outside my comfort zone, I found myself. I started learning about myself as an adult in this world.

Believe me, it wasn't all smooth sailing. I kept a diary and at night, I used to cross off every day that I had survived in my journey to find myself. It was a kind of record of my personal growth and development; a tool that helped me keep a picture of what I was doing to create the person that I am today. If I hadn't gone on this trip to find myself, I believe that I would be a very different person than I am now.

Sometimes you need to change things in your life that are not working and find the courage to make decisions to help you move on and grow. This may mean moving yourself from a comfortable familiar environment to a new one which may seem like an uncomfortable idea. But you don't grow as a person if you always live life in your comfort zone. You don't have to make a massive move like I did but in your own way at some point, you have to be brave to change something in your life.

Remember, we are all a 'work in progress'. When we stop improving and growing, we die a little on the inside and feel stuck or on hold. But quite often, that's self-imposed. Know that you are the person you need, to make yourself grow, to value yourself and feel good about yourself, and to share this with others. Have the courage to release the 'on hold' button and continue to improve and grow. This is within your control and it will allow you to progress.

Know also that you can look for support. Looking for and finding the right support is part of helping yourself and doing that helps you go forward. On this journey of self-improvement, connection with other people is really important. Look for people that will help you progress. This is how we can live together and support each other in this great world we live in today.

WE ALL NEED TO FEEL THAT WE BELONG

Understand that once life becomes a little easier and you become accepted into your community, you as a person have to change the way you think, and learn to cut down some of the barriers that you have built up to protect yourself. This is a form of progression too. Being more open makes it easier to make and keep friends and helps you feel you belong.

Feeling a sense of belonging in a healthy way, makes it way easier to manage fear because while it's still up to you to make the decisions, you won't feel alone, knowing there are people to turn to. Not everyone has an instant supportive family or community, so if this is something missing in your life, start by talking to a person you like. Get the ball rolling. Maybe that person could use your help too. Everyone wants to feel they belong.

FIND YOUR CIRCLE OF SUPPORT

THE COURAGE TO TAKE A CHANCE

Sometimes, when you think about upcoming challenges or new environments, a feeling of fear arises. But it's not always the same fear of being afraid, like being afraid of a bully or a spider. It can feel a little different. It's important to remember that emotions are energy we can't see buzzing around inside our bodies. And with a bit of practice, you can identify different feelings. Sometimes, feelings of fear and excitement feel the same in our body. Sometimes, before we try something new or go into a new environment, we can feel nervous. When the feeling of fear arises, ask yourself, '*Could this be fear or excitement?*' Once you identify whether it's fear or excitement, you have the ability to harness the excitement or step into courage and face your 'fear' head-on.

Fear is not always bad. For example, feeling fear when you try something new is quite normal. When the term "comfort zone" is used, it's because that's where you feel 'comfortable'. If you go outside of that, it's natural to feel new and strange feelings. So when you edge out of your comfort zone to try something new, or meet someone new, you can expect to experience new and often foreign feelings. Sometimes these feelings just can range from feelings of 'unsettled' or 'nervous' or 'stretched' to 'fear' or 'panic'. New feelings like this can make us feel afraid of the unknown.

If you are never pushed out of your comfort zone, you never experience anything new which means you can't progress or change. Sometimes you have to feel slightly uncomfortable to get past your comfort zone and into a new learning or growth zone.

The fear zone has the power to help us. It can be an indicator that we're on the path to our new growth zone. Like in the movies or a book when the characters have to pass through a swamp or dark forest to get to their goal. The ability to walk through the fear zone can bring positive results and make you a more resilient person.

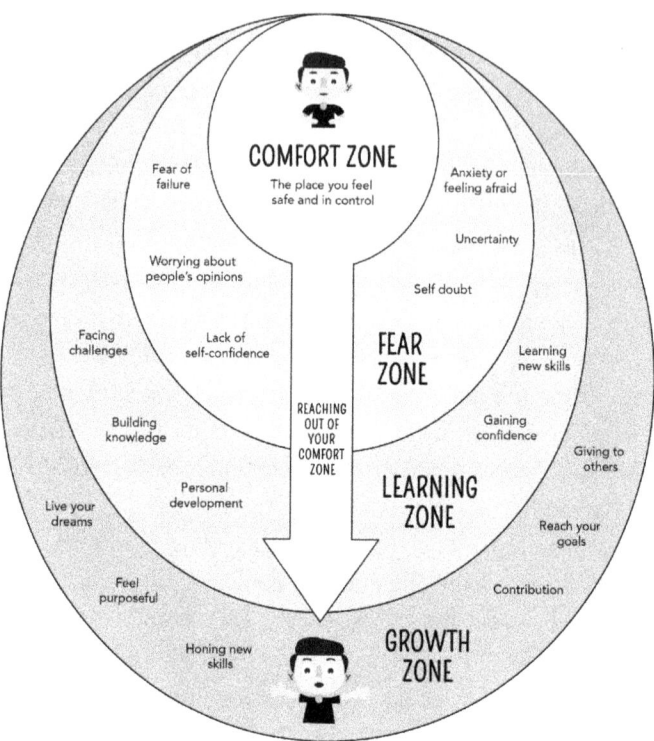

"Once you stop learning, you start dying."
Albert Einstein

When have you taken a chance on yourself
and what was the outcome?

....

....

....

....

....

....

....

....

What did if feel like afterwards?

....

....

....

....

....

DEALING WITH FEAR

Feeling afraid to get outside your comfort zone is a very different feeling to the fear of dealing with a bully. Getting out of your comfort zone can be a nervous but excited type of fear, whereas dealing with bullies triggers our physiological fear (flight or fight response).

When dealing with bullies, many people report feeling helpless and even depressed, and they start doing less and less and start to worry more and more. Some people try to ignore it by watching more TV and start hiding from others. This can lead to the one being bullied becoming more isolated and inactive.

Sometimes fear is easy to see like when you see it on someone's face. But, like the signs of being bullied, the signs of someone in fear can also run deep. Being in fear can raise a lot of different emotions, especially anger, sadness, guilt, shame and depression. It's not fair to live in fear and it isn't right. Bullying must stop.

To release fear it's important to talk to someone you can trust, tell them you feel afraid. You can also confront the bully with a teacher and put rules in place at school.

Learn a new "power skill" like the art of body language or martial arts so you can learn how to walk strong and be powerful.

Learning how to use your voice is also a good thing to do, vocal classes to learn how to raise your voice to say things like *stop, no, go away*.

> "There is no illusion greater than fear."
> Lao Tzu

Are there any small steps you could take to get one foot out of your comfort zone?

....

....

....

....

....

....

....

....

....

....

....

Was there a time when you did something unusual or different and it worked out?

....

....

....

....

....

....

....

....

....

"Kindness is the generous gift
used to help others."

Angie Clucas

CHAPTER 7
A DOGGY SITUATION

"One positive change can help
make you stronger."

Angie Clucas

MIND OVER MATTER

Due to being so small, I have always had a fear of dogs since I was young because when the dogs got excited and jumped up on me, I always got knocked over. Then, just being playful, they'd run over the top of me while I was on the ground. I'd curl up and try and protect myself but when I tried to get up, they'd run straight back over to me because they thought I wanted to play. But in my mind, I just wanted to get the hell away from them and get back inside the house as quickly as possible.

What I was thinking and what the dogs had in mind where two very different ideas, and this same thing happens in our lives a lot of the time between people. We think one thing is being expressed to us but in many cases, we misunderstand what others are trying to tell us. I was sure that the dogs just all had it in for me, and that all they wanted to do was hurt me. In order to cope over the years, I had to change my mindset and started looking at the situation from the dogs' point of view.

I watched the other members of my family playing with our dogs and tried to work out why the dogs were friends with them, but why the same dogs seemed to just be out to pick on me. My family had been giving me tips and advice about this for years, but I never listened. I was just too scared and didn't want anyone telling me what to do. But now I was seeing that my family could be right because they all got along with our dogs just fine.

Once I started listening to what they were saying, I started seeing things from a different point of view. I decided that I needed to find a way to connect with the family dogs in a different way, and not be frightened of them. I needed to come up with some gradual steps to get there.

So, I started by staying inside when the dogs were first let out of their run, to give them time to calm down before I went out there. Then, once they were calmer, I would go outside and stand up against a wall so that when the dogs came up to me, they couldn't knock me over as easily. I also started telling them to "sit" so that they would learn to respect me.

The steps worked. Once I started taking command of the situation, the dogs understood and started showing me respect. Understanding the best way for me to have a friendship with the dogs allowed me to start enjoying their company. This also meant that I became more included in the backyard activities at home which often involved our dogs who were an important part of our family. Building your problem-solving ability not only strengthens your empathy skills (understanding both sides of a situation), it is a valuable skill in life.

Looking back, where have you identified
a problem and what steps did you take to
solve it?

....

....

....

....

....

....

....

....

....

How did you feel afterwards? i.e. confident, happy, etc.

....

....

....

....

....

....

....

....

....

IS THE ONLY THING IN THE WAY, YOU?

If you feel that the only thing that gets in your way is you, you probably ask yourself questions like, "There are always people worse off than me, so what's my problem? Why are these people, who have bigger issues than me, doing so much better than me?"

There are so different answers to those questions, depending who you ask, and you can't ask everyone. So, narrow it down. If you don't know where to start, pick someone that has overcome the same or similar issues that you have, and see what they say, and whether you can follow it. Maybe what they did can work for you, or maybe just parts of it. You can get some good ideas from having a look at how someone else has overcome their problems.

When the only thing that's getting in the way is you, you have two options: start growing or go into hiding. At the point that you realise that this is a choice, the next thing to realise is that the only person that can make this decision is you. Whichever way you go — good or bad — it's up to you to decide. Your choice could mean a change for the better or a change for the worse, but either way, you have to take responsibility for your actions, or lack of action.

OUT WITH BLAME, IN WITH THE NEW

When you stop blaming the world and there's nothing else left to deal with except filling the big empty space that's left, you may feel lost, and have a feeling of needing to fill the void with a new direction.

At this stage, your thoughts and actions could be positive or negative, but if you're here (not blaming anyone anymore), you're probably ready for some positive change. In this new headspace, you may suddenly have nothing to talk about because you've just let go of the familiar old negative 'blaming' thoughts that clouded your thinking. Now, you're at a crossroad and it's time to make a choice: start a new positive path or a new negative one. Which one looks better?

Once you've made the decision to go on a positive path, you can start moving forward because you've chosen to be in a positive mindset. So, the next thing to do is to start making changes: start with some small changes, if you start too big it's too hard on yourself and will set you back into a negative mindset. So, start small. Think of one action that you will do the next day, write it down and put it where you can see it when you first wake up.

You need to remind yourself that this is the first step to having a better life. Use it to start connecting with your new purpose and direction. You can think of these things as you are taking the steps to take back control of your life in a positive way.

GOING ON THE POSITIVE PATH

What is one positive action or step you can take today?

What are some things you could tell yourself to stay inspired and motivated in order to keep stepping forward?

....

....

....

....

....

....

....

....

IT'S OKAY TO MAKE MISTAKES

> "A person who never made a mistake
> never tried anything new."
> **Albert Einstein**

MISTAKES ARE NOT NEGATIVE

This does not mean that you will not make mistakes along the way. In fact, you will, but you'll find it easier as you go along to move more forwards than backwards. This is one reason to start out with small changes, so you can manage your mistakes more easily. But also, so you can gauge and reward yourself for the positive results. To do this, here's an idea:

THE SCOREBOARD FORWARD

Make a scoreboard so that you can have a visual of:

- how many steps forward you are making
- identify when you have bad days and good days.

Look in the interactive book for an explanation of a scoreboard.

MY SCOREBOARD FORWARD
TRACKING MY PROGRESS

OH YEAH! I'M DOING GREAT	OOPS, I'LL KEEP TRYING
ЖHT ЖHT ЖHT	IIII

Recognising both of these is being realistic but still positive. It helps to measure your progress, and makes you feel good. You can over time improve your quality of life. This does not need to involve massive changes because simple and small actions can make huge improvements over a long period of time.

Using your scoreboard can sometimes feel a bit like the game Snakes and Ladders, sometimes you go up and sometimes you slide down. But eventually as you keep climbing you can have more ups than downs.

You can do a mini scoreboard for each day, each week and each month.

You can simply add a point for every time you take a step forward in your life, no matter how small it is, it's good to acknowledge it. And of course, you'll have days where things aren't great, but it's more important to try and have more days where you step up your Ladder of Life than slide down into despair.

Develop the habit of looking at whatever happens through a positive mindset instead of a negative one. One example may be a long-time friend (who always gets 'their way' while you always end up compromising) has decided to move on to another circle of friends. You are unable to change their mind; your only option is to accept their choice and move on with your life. After the sadness leaves, you discover you are happier, you get to do the things you like with friends who respect and honour everyone's choices. Finding the lesson or purpose behind every challenge will help you embrace it instead of fighting it.

Choose not to judge what happens to you. Think of it as everything happens for a reason, and that reason leads you to a greater destiny. Accepting what you don't like happens, acknowledge it's there to teach you something i.e. to push you to grow, and encourage you to make the change you've been asking for. If the same thing keeps showing up, look closer until you find the lesson.

YOUR LADDER OF LIFE

When you take steps forward in your life (and marking them on your scoreboard) you are essentially moving up your Ladder of Life.

You are going from good to greater each time to take a small step.

	5 YEARS
	4.5 YEARS
	4 YEARS
	3.5 YEARS
	3 YEARS
ЖНТ ЖНТ ΙΙ	2.5 YEARS
ЖНТ ЖНТ Ι	2 YEARS
ЖНТ ΙΙΙ	1.5 YEARS
ЖНТ	1 YEAR
ΙΙΙ	6 MONTHS

What backward steps keep appearing on
your scoreboard?

....

....

....

....

....

....

....

....

....

What is the lesson that shows up in these backward steps? Is there a
common theme?

....

....

....

....

....

....

....

....

....

....

What have you done to solve this problem so far?

....

....

....

....

....

....

....

....

....

What strategies can you come up with to diffuse the situations that keep showing up? Think about another angle to tackle this problem: research online what others have done to overcome the same problem.

....

....

....

....

....

....

....

....

Did you make more forward steps than backwards steps? If so, how can you keep your momentum going?

....

....

....

....

....

....

....

....

....

CHANGING YOUR STANDARDS

Our minds are the most powerful tool that we will ever own. Knowing that there is no right or wrong way to accomplish the outcomes you want, but understand that there will always be a way. Knowing your values helps you set your standards and keep your behaviour aligned with what matters to you most.

WHAT ARE VALUES?

Your values are the things that you feel are important in your life. The things that you value the most deep down and determine how you spend and prioritise your time. You can also value things in different situations.

You can have:

Character Values — Character values are the universal values that you need to exist as a good human being.

Family Values — What matters most within your family circle.

Work or school Values — Are values that help you find what you think is most important in school or life and give you satisfaction and purpose.

Personal Values — These are values that you personally put up the top of your values chart. What you find important in life. To help you, here's a short list of personal values. You can mix them around according to your own values.

1. Independence
2. Honesty
3. Courage
4. Creativity
5. Determination
6. Resilience
7. Health
8. Being a good friend
9. Intelligence
10. Kindness
11. Learning
12. Love

Roy E. Disney of Walt Disney Co. said, "When your values are clear to you, making decisions becomes easier."

If you do not value your values, no one else will! Values will help you with your boundaries.

Making decisions around your values removes a lot of the stress about making decisions in the moment. When you make decisions based on your values, the best choice becomes more obvious. Decisions based on your values also gives you more clarity about the consequences of those decisions.

The below activities will help you build the values you wish to guide you.

What qualities do you admire in others? This
could be a friend, family member, celebrity,
sports person, musician, etc.

....

....

....

....

....

....

....

What do you wish to be recognised for by others?

....

....

....

....

....

....

....

....

Write down the values that are important to you, that you wish to live by.

> ★ A list of values can be downloaded from the interactive book at deanpublishing.com/angieclucas ★

....

....

....

....

....

....

....

....

Make a promise to yourself that these values are your new standards to live by for a greater life.

VALUES-BASED VISION BOARD

Next take those values and create a vision board to put up somewhere in your room so you can see them everyday. A picture is worth a thousand words. Create a vision board by cutting out images/words/quotes that align to your values and what you'd like to create and paste on a piece of cardboard, or you can create one online in Canva or Pinterest then print it out. You want to capture the essence of the energy you'd like to have in your life i.e. fun activities, friendships, an item you're saving up for, etc.

You can also place your own set of values on your own 'Tree of Life' — these will help you grow strong and tall.

SHARING YOUR VALUES

This is the start to improving your standards but living by them also involves giving to others. When you share your improved standards in the way you treat others, you improve your personal level of value as well, and this shows in your actions. Actions like these can be very small. For example, just giving someone a smile as you walk past them; saying good morning to someone; opening a door or helping someone with their bag.

These actions have no dollar value, but they can improve another person's day, and in return you will feel good about yourself. It is important to say however, that if your action doesn't get a good response, you must accept that. The actions you take on and the choices you make have consequences which can be either empowering or disempowering. You need to stay within your values. People don't always want help. They may just want some space. Be thoughtful.

And when you make bad choices, remind yourself that wallowing in blame never has ideal outcomes for you, or others around you. Staying 'in blame' just creates negativity and sends you backwards. You have to acknowledge that you made a mistake and learn from it.

Remember, making mistakes is not a negative, it's part of life, but learning from them creates value. When you make constructive choices that bring about a good result, similarly, you should acknowledge these as achievements. Use these experiences to give yourself back the power to make sensible decisions. This will enable you to slowly take control of your life's direction. These actions over time will determine the quality of your future, including who will be your future friends because when you change, your world changes too.

> "When you start going the extra mile
> to encourage life, life will give
> back to you in volumes."
> *Angie Clucas*

How do you know when you are improving your standards?

When you start getting results from lifting your self-esteem. You can see this by starting to look at how you are communicating with other people and comparing yourself with old habits to your new habits.

When you stop playing the blame game and are taking responsibility for your own actions, the scale of your improvement is then measurable by the positive results you achieve. When you work this out for yourself you can then start looking at every section of your life. This is something that you can do one step at a time. These sections could include your friendships, family members, sport team members, partners, workplace, and work colleagues, etc. Once you get this sorted, your growth as a person can take off because you are now more conscious of your environment.

When your standards improve your values increase, as they become very important to you. These new standards will improve your quality of life because you are now demonstrating to the world that you are back in control of your life. When you start going the extra mile to encourage life, life will give back to you in volumes.

The more effort that you put into your environment, the more pleasure and fulfilment you will find. You will start to enjoy every single day because having lifted your standards and brought your values up to a much greater level, you will appreciate things more. This is an ongoing process, a way of life, but it's one you can adopt with joy as you've learnt how to use these tools. And you need to keep reviewing these new skills that you have learnt, so you can keep improving, making sure that you never drop your values and go back to your old habits.

If you find yourself starting to play the blame game, that's your indicator to let you know that you need to sit up and get back on the right track. You must always be honest with yourself — this is the key to gain control over your life.

OUR GOOD FRIEND, INTUITION

Having the gift of intuition can be a real asset. I always listen to my intuition and it has never let me down. Understanding how to use your intuition will help you to make clear and positive decisions when and where you need to. You can use your intuition as a tool to help you live a life where you don't have to be reactive and can manage your emotions, therefore, making more of your life without letting irrational fears take control of your headspace.

There are different ways to recognise the feeling of intuition: some people call it their 'gut' feeling which is exactly what I call it. This is a strong feeling that you 'know it's right' and you feel very strongly about this instinct. You get a sense of knowing that the course of action you are considering is the correct (or incorrect) path moving forward, and that what you're sensing to be true is absolutely true for you. If your intuition is saying "yes" to something you are considering for yourself, you will have a feeling that this will be the most beneficial thing to do for yourself as the person who is experiencing this wonderful intuition, that's you.

> "Never discredit your gut instinct.
> You are not paranoid.
> Your body can pick up on bad vibrations.
> If something deep inside of you says
> something is not right about a
> person or situation, trust it."
>
> **Unkown Author**

When you listen to your intuition, it can help you choose which people you let into your life. Or at least, how much you let people get involved in your life, and the people and things that really matter to you. When you're asking your intuition to kick in about a person, you could ask yourself a question like, *"Would I be happy to introduce this person to my best friend?"* Asking yourself this type of question will help you to tap into the feelings that are coming from your intuition. If you start feeling unsure or uncomfortable, take this as a warning sign — just make some space to think about why you are getting these feelings — this is your intuition saying that maybe this is not the right person to be letting into your life.

Learning to develop a strong sense of intuition is a great skill that with practice, can save you a lot of grief and anxiety. Using your intuition can prevent anxiety which can become very toxic and lack of action can cause you to freeze. For example, just sitting in a chair and overthinking things is really only giving you

> *"The only real valuable thing is intuition."*
> **Albert Einstein**

something to do, that is, think too much. When you overthink things, it can destroy your whole life and take over every thought process. Anxiety is so toxic to our lives. It twists things around and makes you worry and makes everything so much worse than it really is.

GOOD VIBES VERSUS BAD VIBES

Certain people, places and situations can give you 'good vibes' or 'bad vibes'. Just like an animal can detect a predator – we can also detect good situations or bad ones. It takes some practice at first but as you get older it gets easier. We often call good feelings 'good vibes' and say that positive people give us 'good vibes'. We also say that negative or mean people give us 'bad vibes' that is we don't feel good around them. Even places can feel like this. Walking into an old place surrounded by cobwebs and an eerie feeling could be classed as 'bad vibes'.

It's important to start to work with your own 'vibe meter' and feel what makes you feel safe and happy versus what gives you the creeps or 'bad vibes'.

Now, this is not to say that your vibe meter is always accurate but it's important to listen to your own inner instincts and if a situation or person doesn't feel right to you – then listen to that.

I will give you an example. You are standing alone waiting for an elevator and the doors open, inside is a man that looks a little dishevelled with a shoe missing and messy hair. He doesn't make eye-contact with you. Your vibe meter says "don't go in" but you don't want to offend him, you don't want him to feel that you think he's a creep, so you ignore your vibe meter and go in. Was that the right choice? Of course not! You cared about a stranger's feelings and ignored your own.

This however is an easy example, it's not as easy when you meet someone who appears nice and wears nice clothes and says all the right things. But it's important to listen to your vibe meter. If your body is signalling something to you...then listen to it. That person, situation or scenario may be best left alone if you feel 'bad vibes'.

I try to surround myself with things, places and people that help me feel good. Positive friends and environments help our mental and physical health and wellbeing.

List people, places and situations that give you good vibes and
bad vibes.

GOOD VIBES   BAD VIBES

What are the signs in your body that signal
your gut feeling or intuition?

....

....

....

....

....

....

....

List 3 occasions where you made a decision based on your gut feeling
or intuition — what was the outcome?

....

....

....

....

....

....

....

....

....

....

....

List a time when you ignored your gut feeling or intuition — what
was the outcome?

....

....

....

....

....

....

....

....

KEEPING AN OPEN MIND

In life, it's good to keep an open mind. The difference between an
open mind and a closed mind is that open-minded people tend to
allow more possibilities into their lives, whereas close-minded people
often shut the door to change and stay rigid in their beliefs. Having
an open your mind allows you to be curious and explore more
questions about your life.

CHARACTERISTICS OF OPEN-MINDED PEOPLE

- They are curious to new ideas
- They are open to hear other people's input
- They feel empathy for others
- Are happy to explore a new possibility
- They believe others have a right to share their beliefs and thoughts
  (if they're not harming anyone)
- They don't bully or get angry about people's differences
- They are receptive to a wider variety of information
- They listen to other people's point of view.

Being open-minded allows you to take in a variety of information in order to think critically and rationally about it. It can also help you think more creatively. For example, when you have an idea that you are passionate about, it can really change your life as it can get you excited. You start thinking about projects and good ideas, and you stop thinking about the sad and bad things. This type of thinking is creative and can be transformative.

Being open-minded to changing your thought patterns can help get you out of a negative headspace — a headspace that you may have been in without even knowing the effect it was having on you. The effort of changing the way you think is often uncomfortable because you have to step into unfamiliar thought patterns. But we become so much more by putting ourselves out — as long as you are safe — into the world of possibility.

Remember, safety zone and comfort zone are two different things.

If you keep an open mind to exploring new possibilities in your life, you'll start to welcome new people and new experiences into your life and getting out of your comfort zone will seem like an opportunity, not a fear. This is when you really start to grow and develop your emotional and mental strength.

Having an open mind doesn't mean that you accept everything and don't use your own judgement and discernment. You should always think critically and keep your wits about you. Having an open mind is being flexible enough to explore new options. It allows you to be more POSITIVE and have PLENTY more opportunities. That's why I call it the Positive Plenty Mindset.

THE CLOSED MIND

If you have a closed mind to things in life then life will close itself off to you too. For example, if you make a point-blank statement, that same idea cannot work, it shuts the door on any creative thought processes that could have come up around that idea. In this type of thinking, there's no way the idea can work or be implemented because there's no room for thinking about it in any positive or creative ways. If I had of told myself, "I can never write a book," then you wouldn't be holding this book in your hands. It was only because I opened my mind to the possibility and had some good support people around me who encouraged me to write, that this became a reality. Don't shut yourself off from good things or good ideas.

If you turn every good idea into a negative statement, then you will create a headspace of negative thoughts. In this negative headspace, you slowly close your world down and don't let new insights or opportunities expand.

When this happens, you can become NEGATIVE and decrease your possibilities to NOUGHT. That's why I call it the Negatively Nought Mindset.

Life can change just by gradually changing your thought patterns and by taking the time to recognise when you are closing the door to your mind. You must take the leap from Negatively Nought to Positively Plenty.

When you recognise you are closing your mind's door, ask yourself: "What else is possible here that I haven't considered?" or "What opportunities exist here that I haven't explored yet?"

This will shift the energy and get you out of Negatively Nought and into Positively Plenty.
- Negatively Nought gives you nothing.
- Positively Plenty gives you possibility.

Life is always changing and challenging, sometimes like a rollercoaster with its ups and downs, but it's your responsibility to take control of yours. You can change the way you look at life and once you do, life starts looking different. This might mean letting go of some emotions that may have become excuses to shut down, like guilt, pain or rejection. Letting go of excuses creates the space to deal with whatever comes your way.

Some excuses you could let go of are:

....

....

....

....

....

....

....

....

....

....

"Experience grows your confidence
one step at a time."
Angie Clucas

DEALING WITH WHO YOU ARE

No one person on this earth has all the elements of an idyllic 'perfect' life. There is no human being that is perfect in this way. Even though at times you may see someone that looks close to that ideal, they are not perfect, no one is.

Every single one of us has our own challenges in life, so you're definitely not the only one! Just think how boring life would be if there were no challenges. You need challenges to make life interesting and to be able to grow, to become your best self. Accept yourself as unique. This is the reason why we are all dealt different cards — we are usually dealt the cards that we have the capability to handle, even if most of the time it doesn't feel that way.

THE TWO-WAY MIRROR

There are reasons why we connect with certain people and why particular people start appearing in our lives. The world outside of you can see you in a much different way to how you see yourself, another lesson that's important to understand. When a new person enters your life, ask yourself the question, "Why? For what reason or purpose has this happened?" Think about what you may learn from this person by getting to know them and the value brought into your life by spending time with them.

It's not a one-way process; these lessons are there for both individuals. This is how we grow from connecting with other people and having new experiences in life. Human beings are information gatherers. That's how we keep moving forward. When we stop learning new things, our world start to shrink.

When you start to recognise another person's qualities as standing out — for example, you might start seeing them as honest, considerate, generally happy, angry or sad — in most cases the qualities that stand out to you, stand out because there is some level of these qualities within yourself. You might be aware of it or you might not, but the things you see in someone else are usually things that you already have or want to change within yourself.

BEING YOU

To make the best of the world you live in, first try to become comfortable with yourself. Trust in your ability to proudly live day-to-day as your own unique identity in the environment or society in which you live. Being happy within yourself in knowing that you are always working on improving yourself helps you deal with challenges that present themselves on a daily basis.

You and only you can decide which actions you are going to take in navigating your way through life. I personally decided at a very young age that I was going to live my life in a positive way and not let the cards that I had been dealt with be a negative influence on my future. Not for one minute am I saying that this was easy, but it did give me the foundation to deal with events that were to come into my life moving forward, like the bullying that I suffered and to a lesser degree still endure today.

Growing up as a very small person I had more than my share of obstacles to deal with. Just starting school was a minefield for me. I was exposed to so many kids that didn't understand my uniqueness. They didn't understand the reason why I looked different to them and for the first time in my life because I was at school, I didn't have the protection of my family around. This was something that I never would have been able to handle if I didn't think of myself as unique. People often think of 'different' as bad. It's not. It's just another word for 'unique'.

There is a fine line between going into survival mode and starting to mirror the behaviour of the people that are bullying you. I had to learn this lesson very young as I soon recognised that mirroring other's actions was not sitting comfortably with who I was inside. It lowered my sense of self-worth and did not line up with my values and standards.

I could have had a very different outlook on these issues by just running away and not facing up to the situations that I found myself in; situations that happened almost every morning tea and lunchtime that I was at school until I was about fifteen years old when finally, as people got to know me, I started being respected at school for the person that I am.

The attitudes that you decide to apply to your life steer your direction, and your ability to endure conflict and issues as they arise. Believe me, it's is not always easy to change your attitude and direction but at least you have better control of the outcomes long-term. You must become strong and over time as you practice, your character will develop much quicker than those that don't. You will have a better sense of self-worth. People that go through shit in their lives usually end up growing as a person with much more understanding than those who just sail through life with very few challenges.

> *"I personally decided at a very young age that I was going to live my life in a positive way and not let the cards that I had been dealt with be a negative influence on my future."*
>
> **Angie Clucas**

CAUSE AND EFFECT

If you come across people that think it's great to tease you just to entertain their egos, remember that these people always have underlying issues of their own. Their actions towards you are a result of them not dealing with the pain or grief that they have inside, and then targeting it on someone, in this case you. For every effect there is always a cause (it's even scientific!) even if you can't see it or understand it at any particular moment in time.

But the cause of bullying is in the bully,
not the one being bullied.

Remember we are all on this earth for just a moment in time, so make the most of yours and create the best version of yourself, because you'll never get that time back once it's gone.

You can spend your life saying things like, "Poor me", or do what I did; make the choice to make very day count, change your environment if you need to, and try to help as many people as possible that make their way into your life. Never expect anything in return because that is not what life's about. Knowing that you are able to help someone every day is reward enough. You don't have to do massive things and they may not need your help. It's more about reaching out with a friendly attitude. Doing something simple like opening a door for someone or just taking the time to say good morning to a person that you pass in the street.

Simple actions like these can have great benefits to both you and other people. It lifts everyone's spirits, and as this repeats, little-by-little, makes our world a better place to live in. Then, more and more people will see each other's kind actions over time, creating momentum to heal parts of our society that are lost in negativity. This momentum can educate younger people without even having to tell them what to do, as they'll experience it all around them and learn that good behaviour is normal.

We must all lead by example. Change always starts with someone's action and we all learn from following or copying someone or something. So, when you see a need for positive change, why should it not be you that leads the way in your part of this world?

I believe that the best way for me to feel empowered is to leave a legacy behind that others can learn from; even if it's just one thing from me that has changed their outlook on life for the better.

I'd like to share a story of an inspiring young man from the Northern Territory called Angus Copelin-Walters. The day I met this young boy I knew he was a very special kid, he has a heart of gold. When I first met Angus in 2015 his mum told me that he was having a rough time at school because he was dyslexic. She asked me if I could have a chat with him because she had some concerns about how he was coping. It turns out that the other students were giving him a hard time because he was a little different to them when it came to processing information and writing.

We had a great chat and became good friends. I gave him some advice and we still keep in touch. He feels comfortable to open up to me because he knows that I understand what it's like to be a little different.

Anyway, Angus decided to start his own business making Croc Candy. It is the coolest brand ever: he makes things like Croc eye lollipops and Rock Candy. So, one morning we spent time together and I showed him how to count money and work out the costs of producing a product and then the steps required to make a profit. With the help of his very supportive family, at the ripe age of ten, his business Croc Candy is going gangbusters. Mr Croc Candy is kicking goals beyond his dreams. He has appeared on TV including 'Weekend Sunrise' and the 'Today Extra' show as well as radio and magazine and newspapers including *Woman's Day* and *The Herald Sun*. Not to mention that Mr Croc Candy was exclusively interviewed by Prime Minister Scott Morrison about his entrepreneurship and attitude. When the Prime Minister asked Angus about the key to his success, he replied "just trying". I believe that to be true in life, sometimes that's all it takes to turn your entire life around — just trying.

I know one of his heroes is Richard Branson who also has dyslexia but I think Richard Branson may have some competition with the way Angus's business is going. It's skyrocketing and I'm super proud of him.

Go to: **deanpublishing.com/angieclucas** to see the interview. Or visit Angus's website at **croccandy.com** for more information.

MR CROC CANDY
WRITING TO HIS
FRIEND SCOTT
MORRISON
TO UPDATE
HIM ABOUT
CROC CANDY'S
PROGRESS

Photo credit: Angus Copelin-Walters, Croc Candy

MR CROC CANDY
WITH HIS FRIEND
SCOTT MORRISON

Photo credit: Angus Copelin-Walters, Croc Candy

DON'T TELL ME I CAN'T

The worst thing someone can say to me is, "You're too short, you can't do that."

In my life, 'can't' is not in my vocabulary. This word can be so destructive to your headspace, creating a negative attitude which can lead to giving up on yourself.

As a kid, I was raised to not let my stature be an excuse. I was told that I was able to achieve anything that I put my mind to. I live by that rule. There is always a way to achieve what you want to achieve, but you must be willing to look outside the square because sometimes you need to. When someone says to me that something can't happen for no good reason, in my experience it's often because they haven't looked at all possible options. The expression 'never say never' is of great value to use because it helps you achieve, when others are too lazy to try new things.

When you use a positive mindset, you can help empower others to start thinking more positively too. This helps stop a culture of negativity and helps create good self-esteem, enabling you to move forward. At the point where you take full responsibility for your life, you become in control of your actions and therefore the direction in which you will go. You can choose to experience the most of what life has to offer.

I will never live my life seeing myself as a victim, as that finishes badly, and ends up in the 'poor me' life which never has a happy ending. When you let the past consume your headspace it results in a non-productive life as you are always living in the past, never looking at the choices in front of you; choices that are waiting for you to grab with both hands and turn into results that you can be proud of.

When you have self-control and are focused on the present, you respond differently. There are no issues around second-guessing yourself as you are confident to follow your instincts and trust your feelings. In this kind of mindset, you can be honest with yourself. Then, you are able to say what you mean and mean what you say. This will build your reputation up to a high standard and people will believe your word. Your word is a very important personal commitment that will always be true when you live by honest values.

Making the decision that no one is responsible except you for your life, means that you never have to live by someone else's expectations. You don't need to build a wall around you to protect yourself due to not having the confidence to say, "No" to others that suck the energy out of you. The wrong people in your life can drain your self-worth and slowly bring you to your knees over a period of time.

By building your own resilience, you can be empowered to live the most rewarding and fulfilled life with less regrets. You can enjoy the adventures that come your way, because you are now strong enough to say, "Yes" to new pathways that can lead to an exciting lifetime of value-based experiences.

PEOPLE WHO WERE TOLD THEY COULDN'T DO IT... UNTIL THEY DID:

A lot of amazing people were criticised or told they could never do something...until they did. I was always told by others that I was too short to do things, like drive a car or be a mum. People think that my syndrome stops me from living fully. But it doesn't. I have just discovered new ways to do things that's all.

My inspiration Einstein didn't start speaking until he was four years old and didn't read until he was seven. People thought that he was dumb or mentally handicapped. But he ended up being one of the world's greatest scientists and won a Nobel Prize. So much for being dumb, hey?

But it wasn't just Einstein, so many people have been told they weren't able to do or be something.

The whole reason we have lightbulbs in our home is because of a guy named Thomas Edison. Growing up he was told by his teachers that he was 'too stupid to learn anything'. He ended up becoming a great inventor and had more than 1,000 patents, including the phonograph and electric lamp to his name.

. . .

Hollywood icon Steven Spielberg is known for his amazing movies. He is a movie producer, director and screenwriter. But many don't know that he was rejected by the University of Southern California's School of Cinematic Arts — not once, but twice!

. . .

The famous writer J.K Rowling wasn't always famous. Before her first Harry Potter book she was feeling down. She had no money, was depressed and divorced. She was struggling on welfare as a single mum whilst writing her first novel. Thank god she didn't let her mental demons get in the way of her creative passion.

. . .

Walt Disney invented Disneyland. How cool and magical is that place? Before he did that he worked for a newspaper editor who said that he "lacked imagination and had no good ideas." Can you believe that? No good ideas! Well as you know he went on to create the best idea ever!

. . .

Ever heard of the Dyson vacuum cleaner? Well the guy that invented it James Dyson tried for 15 years to invent it. He had 5,126 failed prototypes. He was often told to give up but he didn't. He went on to create the best-selling bagless vacuum cleaner which led to a net worth of nearly 5 billion dollars.

Layne Beachley was small, not as small as me but still small. When she was a child she found out that she was adopted and it made her feel worthless. She really loved surfing and the waves helped her cope with feelings of depression and suicide. She set her sights on becoming a world champion surfer and she made it. She won seven world titles. But it was the change in her heart that was the most rewarding. By acknowledging her battles and asking for help, Layne Beachley found inner peace and happiness. She still loves surfing.

. . .

Nick Vujicic was born in 1982 with no arms and no legs. Throughout his childhood he suffered bullying and ridicule, and he tried to end his own life. Some people thought that he would spend his life feeling depressed and relying on others. But that is the opposite of what he did. Thankfully he didn't take his life and is now a hugely successful motivational speaker. He has spoken to millions of people worldwide and inspires people wherever he goes. When people tell him he can't do something...he says, "Watch me". To check out Nick and his experiences with bullying, just search "Nick Vujicic Bullying" and you'll hear his inspiring story.

. . .

Ever heard of the name Aaron "Wheelz" Fotheringham? He is one of the most famous skaters in the world. But he has one little difference – he skates in a wheelchair. When he was in school some teachers thought he should go into the disabled PE class and of course, some people didn't think he could be a "skater". But he always believed in himself and fought to join 'normal' PE class. You should see him: he flips, he does tricks, he somersaults, he is awesome. He even made the first somersault in wheelchair history. He never listened to what other people thought he was capable of, he just went out there and lived his own dreams.

Check his story out on: **aaronfotheringham.com**

"Everybody is a genius. But if you judge a fish by its ability to climb a tree, it will live its whole life believing that it is stupid."

Albert Einstein

Chapter 8

BE AN UPSTANDER, NOT A BYSTANDER

"Look in the mirror, that's the person to make you better."

Angie Clucas

BULLYING
IS NEVER OKAY!

When I was growing up, bullying fell into three categories:

1. Verbal — name calling, teasing, being put down, and threatening to harm another.

2. Social — spreading rumours, playing horrible jokes, leaving someone out on purpose, embarrassing someone in public.

3. Physical — hitting, punching, kicking, spitting, tripping or pushing.

These days, technology has transformed our lives: the internet, use of smartphones and social media are a part of our daily habits and extends well beyond the end of the school or workday. And with this, cyberbullying has emerged.

Technology means bullying is no longer confined to schoolyards or street corners. Cyberbullying can happen anywhere and anytime of day, images and rumours can be spread far more quickly than they can in person, and there is a sense of anonymity for the bully due to the physical distance from the victim.

Cyberbullying behaviour may include:

- **Exclusion** — the deliberate act of leaving a person out from an online group or conversation on purpose.
- **Harassment** — offensive, abusive and hurtful messages repeatedly online, by text or email.
- **Outing/Doxing** — when a bully distributes personal information to publicly humiliate the victim. This can be in the form of pictures, videos or text and is shared publicly without permission, and includes the use of 'sexting' and sexually explicit material.
- **Fraping** — when someone logs into a person's account and posts inappropriate content with their name which has the potential to be harmful by ruining their reputation.
- **Masquerading** — where a bully creates a fake identity to harass someone anonymously. The bully can impersonate someone else to send malicious messages.
- **Dissing** — refers to the act of a bully spreading cruel information about their target through public posts or private messages to either ruin their reputation or relationships with other people.
- **Trolling** — the deliberate act of provoking a response through the use of insults on online forums and social networking sites. Trolls spend their time looking for arguments.
- **Flaming** — similar to trolling but will usually be a more direct attack on a victim to incite them into online fights.
- **Cyberstalking** — Cyberstalking is a serious form of cyberbullying that can extend to threats of physical harm to the person being targeted. It can include monitoring, false accusations, threats, and is often accompanied by offline stalking.

Let's look at facts. There are 3,893,834 students across Australia — three out of five students (59%) have experienced bullying — that's 2.3 million students! Types of bullying experienced by those who have been bullied include:

- 50% verbal bullying
- 20% physical bullying
- 13% via social media
- 11% via text message
- 6% other (social exclusion, gossiping, emotional/mental).

1 in 7 students who are bullied do not speak to anyone (14%) — that's 340,656 students in Australia who stay silent. Bullied students who speak up are most likely to talk to parents (27%) and friends (24%).[1]

Beyond Blue[2] help many people that struggle with bullying and mental health problems. They talk to teenagers every day about tough issues like bullying, self-harm, eating disorders, anxiety and feeling suicidal.

Some people still don't get it. Some people don't understand that words are like weapons and they hurt. Something happened a couple of years ago that made me want to increase my own voice and step up and speak out loudly about the impact of bullying.

One Saturday morning in 2018, I was scrolling my Facebook page and came across a post the ABC had posted about Amy "Dolly" Everett. My heart dropped. I knew this young woman's beautiful face — she was once the face of iconic Australian hat company Akubra. She had a ripper smile and everyone loved her. Everyone that is except her bullies. She had been silently facing a hidden torment: relentless and cruel bullying and cyberbullying.

---

1   Fell, Ashley. Mccrindle: mccrindle.com.au "Research reveals shocking new statistics of Australia's bullying crisis." Published online September 2020. https://mccrindle.com.au/insights/blog/three-in-five-australian-students-have-experienced-bullying/ McCrindle is a partner of https://makebullyinghistory.org

2   https://www.beyondblue.org.au

During summer, on January 3 2018, Dolly took her own life. She was only 14 years old.

Sadness filled my entire body, this beautiful angel was gone…all because of other people's cruelty.

I knew only too well the feelings of being bullied and it can drive even the most resilient people to the edge. Like me, Dolly also lived in the Northern Territory and it hit me like a tonne of bricks. She had the rest of her life ahead of her but it was tragically cut short because of other people's cruelty.

I decided that I needed to step up and try to help these young people, to teach them that what they were going through was rough and help them find ways through without succumbing to suicide. I needed to show them that taking their own lives was not the answer and there are other things they could like finding the right person to talk to and getting help.

I instantly replied to the ABC's post and offered to talk about the effects of bullying. I had to do something. They thought that my message was spam and replied back asking me to not 'spam' them. This made me more determined to do something, I knew I had to speak up so I rang their office and told them I wasn't spam but a person who had been bullied and wanted to stop more of it happening. They said someone would call me back in ten minutes.

True to their word, I received a phone call back from the ABC and I went on to explain how I was writing a chapter in a book called *Resilience: Building a Powerful Mindset*[3] and had made a video of my anti-bullying message because I wanted to let young people know that I understand what they are going through and that there is a light at the end of tunnel from being bullied. The ABC interviewed me and that night I made National news. They used some of my video for their story too.[4]

---

3   *Resilience: Building a Powerful Mindset*, Dean Publishing. Macedon, Australia. 17 October 2017.

4   Wellington, Shahni. ABC News. "Territorians share stories of bullying, offer advice and hope for help." Published online Monday 15th January, 2018.

Territorians share stories of bullying, offer advice and hope for help

By Shahni Wellington and staff

Posted Mon 15 Jan 2018 at 10.58am, updated Mon 15 Jan 2018 at 12.51pm

Angela Clucas is now the manager of Darwin's aviation museum, after first working as the cleaner. (ABC News: Shahni Wellington)

Now, I can tell you that I'm not one for putting myself out into the media because I want to see my face on telly. It had nothing to do with that. The reason I keep talking about it, writing books about it, contacting people about it is because it's critical. There are young lives at stake and I'm going to do absolutely everything in my power to stop bullying and help people live happy and bully-free. As Dolly's message advocates "Speak, even if your voice shakes." And that's what I'm doing Dolly and will continue to do.

Interestingly, after that small stint on TV a lady that knew called me. She told me that her grandson Sam didn't want to go to school because of bullies. I immediately sent her my video and she passed it on to the Sam's Mum.

When Sam got home from school that day his mum sat down with him and they watched the video together. He had tears running down his face as he realised he wasn't the only person that had to deal with being bullied. Instantly, he didn't feel alone. This can be a powerful mindset shift because often when you're being bullied, you can feel incredibly alone and think that it's only happening to you.

The next morning Sam was totally different. He was the first one to be ready to leave the house and he felt he had some new tools to deal with bullies. Today Sam enjoys school and has a bright future ahead. This makes me so proud as I know that when I listened to Dolly's message and decided to speak out, that I have been able to save a young person from having a sad experiences during their school life. This is Dolly's legacy too.

In the wake of Dolly's death, her family set up "Dolly's Dream" to raise awareness around bullying and harassment. 15-year-old Charlotte McLaverty created a video on the impact of cyberbullying for Dolly's Dream. Check it out on Dolly's Dream website at **dollysdream.org.au**.

There are many useful resources on this website for parents, teens and kids.

Daniel Donahoo, the Senior Advisor for Dolly's Dream wrote:
Cyberbullying thrives because children and young people don't feel capable of sharing their experience. It happens on the couch while your brother plays video games, at the table with your family, in private spaces at home, on the bus, in the schoolyard with friends. Cyberbullying happens even when there are the people who can help you sitting right beside you. The reasons for not sharing may be multiple and varied: a fear of admitting you are being bullied, threats from the cyberbully, culture of trying to just "deal with it yourself", scared someone will take your technology away.[5]

---

5 Donahoo, Daniel. "Are your words doing damage: how to talk to your teen and help stop cyber bullying." Published online September 24 2019. https://parenthub.dollysdream.org.au/are-your-words-doing-damage

I think one of the most important and necessary messages I have ever heard is Dolly's message of **"Be Kind"**. That's all it takes to turn this entire bullying landscape around – people being kind.

> *"In a world where you can be anything — be kind."*
> **Caroline Flack**

WHAT CAN I DO?

There's some really good advice at esafety.gov.au about how to stay safe and what to do about online bullying. Here are some things they suggest[6]:

- If you see bullying behaviour online (and offline), don't let it slide, speak up. There are a number of ways to take action and go from being a bystander to an upstander.
- DM your friend — check in to see if they are okay and remind them how awesome they are.
- Call it out — if you feel confident and safe, stand up to the person doing the bullying and make it clear what they're doing is wrong. It can be as simple as commenting *Thumbs down emoji*, or your negative emoji of choice, or NOT COOL on the mean post can get your point across.
- Get extra help — if your friend seems really down, withdrawn or skipping school, you can talk to a trusted adult or teacher, or refer them to a counsellor or support service to talk to a counsellor anonymously online (refer

---

6   eSafety Commissioner. "Be an upstander — not a bystander." Retrieved online October 2020. https://www.esafety.gov.au/young-people/be-an-upstander-not-a-bystander

back to the youth resources in Chapter 1).

- Help your friend report cyberbullying — do your bit to make the internet a more positive place and report posts online that are intentionally trying to hurt someone. Make sure you screenshot evidence and information before blocking/deleting/reporting to the social media site or app and encourage your friend to report it as well to help it get taken down faster.

REPORTING CYBERBULLYING

If you or someone you know is experiencing cyberbullying, and is under the age of 18, your first step is to advise parents and teachers, so they are aware what is happening. You can report cyberbullying to the eSafetyCommisioner in Australia. You will need to collect relevant evidence and information before you make a report, you can view the steps to make a complaint at **esSafety.gov.au**.

If you would like to talk to a counsellor refer back to the youth resources in Chapter 1.

"Stand up, speak even if your voice shakes."
Amy "Dolly" Everett

Chapter 9

VEGIES WITH A GRAIN OF SALT

*"When you are strong within yourself,
you will then be happy."*

Angie Clucas

WHEN ONE DOOR CLOSES ANOTHER OPENS

After 4½ years servicing the outstations it was time for new adventures. With money saved from Oenpelli, I purchased a house in Darwin. The plan was to take a month off while I worked out what I wanted to do. With the changeover of workers between Oenpelli and Darwin every 2–3 months, I had a base of people I knew, and both my parents and my godparents had also moved to Darwin.

I arrived into Darwin at six o'clock Sunday night, and my friend asked me what I had planned for Monday. My only plans at that stage were unpacking my ute. They said, "I've got a job for you, part time, and you start at nine o'clock tomorrow morning". I went and checked it out and ended up working the mornings in the office of the cleaning company, the afternoons cleaning in the new Parliament House followed by a school on the way home. I started getting to know people with the same work ethic as myself (one of my values) and friendships grew from there. I worked six days a week, weekend down time was catching up with friends at bbqs at their place, setting up my yard and planting plants.

Looking for more freedom I set up my own business, a smoko food and drink van called "The Little Visitor" and visited construction sites, new subdivisions and workplaces. I put on a second van which Mum drove for me. The days were long, from four am to six pm. Eventually I shut down the businesses and went back to work in operations for the airport shuttle, coordinating buses, hotel pickups and drop offs, and worked nights. I was working the night the Twin Towers in New York (9/11) was hit, and the night Ansett collapsed operations in Australia.

I'd been in operations close to four years when I ended up taking a weekend off. One of my friend's was going on a blind date to a rodeo and she conned me into going with her because she didn't want to go by herself. The bloke she was meeting had the same idea and he'd encouraged his mate Gary into going. They didn't end up together, but we did. Gary had his own construction business as a grader operator, and had similar values to me — we're both really big on persistence, if it doesn't work then you find another way. We'd both grown up in country towns, we weren't city slickers. When I told my boss I'd met Gary, she told me laughing, "no more weekends off."

A year later I ended up at the doctors thinking I was getting kidney stones again, and unbeknownst to me, the doctor did a pregnancy test. The doctor rang me at work to tell me I was pregnant. It was a pretty big shock as I'd been told in my early 20s I wouldn't be able to have kids (actually it was only then I was diagnosed with Russell Silver syndrome after an emergency hospital trip from Oenpelli to Darwin). But here I was at 31 years of age, 16 weeks pregnant and it turned out with only 4 months to work things out; but the baby had other ideas. A month before my due date I ended up at the hospital in the early hours of Sunday morning coughing up blood. At first they told me it was preeclampsia, but it turned out the baby had cracked my sternum as well. It then took them until just before noon on Tuesday to work out how they were going to get the baby out of me.

Silvia was born on the 19 June 2001 weighing 5lb 11oz (2.5kg) and 59cm long — a beautiful healthy, normal-sized girl. The day after she was born, stitched back up, my body battered, I wandered down to the nursery in agony to see her. I couldn't hold Silvia incase the stitches ruptured, and I couldn't bathe her because I couldn't reach the bathtub. The second time I wanted to see Silvia they brought her to me in bed. With Silvia lying on the bed next to me and with nobody around, I said, "I've got no idea what I'm doing kid, it could be a rough ride, but we'll see how we go."

That's how I dealt with life in general, as a problem arises, you deal with it. As long as you've got faith in yourself, you can work through almost anything.

Shopping with a newborn was a challenge. I dreaded going to the shops. If I was feeling down or tired, these types of trips could become overwhelming. I was used to people staring at me when I went to the shops, but when I became a mother this became more prevalent. So now, like any mum, I was pushing my gorgeous girl around in pram stopping sometimes to pick her up or comfort her. It could be hard trying to get things off the shelves and juggle a baby. I spent many shopping sprees only buying from the first few shelves from the bottom because I didn't want to ask anyone for help and draw even more attention to myself. Of course, some baby items aren't stacked on the bottom shelves and often I had no choice but to ask for assistance.

People seemed to be shell-shocked at what they were seeing: a child-sized woman being a mother! People of all ages, parents and kids would point us out. Even as a small baby she covered a huge portion of my upper body and some people literally stopped in their tracks to stare at us.

But for me, going shopping with my daughter was a normal part of life, but I was really 'over' the reactions I was getting from the general public. I felt like a sideshow to people and I had to learn how to cope with the extra attention now I had a baby with me.

Then, one day, when my daughter was a little bit older and was able to ask me questions, she said, "Why do people point at you Mum? And why are they laughing at us when we're not doing anything funny?"

That day was the day I decided that I had to help Silvia understand. It needed to come from me, and it needed to be now because now was when she was asking. I needed to go and sit down with her while we were in this environment and explain to her the reasons this was happening because it was starting to affect her as well. This was the best way I could answer her and support her, and it was my responsibility.

By doing this and following my instincts to talk to my daughter then and there, I gained a lot of clarity as well, which I was then able to pass on to her: as I started my explanation, I became sharply aware — it wasn't the children's fault for pointing and laughing at me all these years. It was because their parents or carers hadn't been able to explain to them why I was so small. They hadn't told their kids that behind every person that looks 'different' in appearance, there are usually reasons for it that are out of that person's control. The taunting children didn't know any better because they had not been shown anything else.

In the middle of this experience, I was able to talk to my daughter in a way that she understood and could feel okay with. Silvia and I both gained a great life lesson that day which will stay with us forever.

FINDING A REPLY

Finding a reply to people who give you a hard time about your appearance can be tricky. It helps if you have a think about how you can reply in a positive way without making yourself feel bad.

When a young child comes up to me in a shopping centre or other public place and starts pointing at me and telling everyone within hearing distance that I am short, I know that they have not been educated yet about how to treat people who look different in appearance.

I get upset on the inside when that child is holding hands with the adult that's looking after them and that adult says nothing about it to the child. This lack of action does not teach the child that it is rude to display such behaviour and that it can hurt the person's feelings. They don't understand the damage it can do to a person's self-esteem over a long period of time.

EDUCATING KIDS TOGETHER

In these kinds of situations, if adults don't have these skills to educate their children, I ask that they be brave enough to ask the adult in front of them being teased to assist. They'll usually be grateful that you have asked them for help. It shows respect and acknowledges that fact that they are the expert in this situation because they live with these issues on a daily basis. It also shows the child a better way to deal with someone who looks different.

Children need guidance from the adults in their life to become more respectful towards others. Kids should know, like the rest of us, that everyone in this world needs a chance to live their life to the best of their ability and to be able to be part of the general community. Adults need to be comfortable enough to deal with explaining to the younger generation about how to deal with others. Prejudice based on appearance is a problem and if we don't deal with it, nothing will change from one generation to another.

I've found myself in this predicament so many times that I found I wanted a response up my sleeve to help everyone deal with what's always an uncomfortable situation. I chose humour as my tool. So, now when I get a chance to talk to a child that asks me the question, "Why are you so small?"

I say "This is what happens when you don't eat your vegies! So, when Mum or Dad put vegies on your dinner plate, you better eat them. Otherwise, you might end up like me!" This surprises the kids and the adults, and makes the kids think more about the food they eat! It also gives me a way out of having to deal with any more teasing from the child.

I feel like I have achieved something when this happens because this child and adult walk away with a different mindset, and I believe it causes them to think twice about their actions moving forward in how to deal with people like me; people who look different. I get a sense of accomplishment from having this type of experience. When this happens, I feel like I'm making a difference, making this world a better place to live in for all.

THE OTHER SIDE OF THE FENCE

I'd like people to remember — and especially people who may be naïve as to how to treat people that, for example, look like me — that from my side of the fence, I am always working on becoming the best version of myself that I can be. And, if we all work on our own best versions of ourselves, together we can make our world a much better place to live in.

You must come up with ways to deal with situations that become constant issues in your life otherwise they can start to get to you. Living with constantly painful issues can easily consume your mind and over time gets you down which in turn, can impact your health and your way of life. Remember, every life is valuable, and we all have lessons to learn from each other. And one of those lessons is to respect each other's differences.

MANAGING PEOPLE AT WORK

When Silvia started school, I started working at The Australian Aviation Heritage Centre. After having run childcare at home for the past 3 ½ years I was after a job with no responsibility, however that didn't last long. They asked me if I could use a till (a computerised till), and I hadn't used a computer before. But after a day, the till turned out to be alright, so I shifted to a split role of half cleaning and half counter work. From there I worked my way from cleaner to manager.

As the manager of Darwin Aviation Museum (DAM), I want all of our customers to have a great experience when they visit our museum. So, when a bus tour group pulls up, I make sure that a staff member always greets them as they arrive to make them feel welcome. This is what I call good customer service, but it does come at a cost, on a personal level.

I've had tour bus customers tell me that I am very short, just in case I didn't know this fact already. I also get told that they think I am sitting down when I am serving behind the counter and that I am rude for not showing them the respect of standing up when serving them as customers. I usually tell these people "thank you for your observations" and leave the conversation at that. Most of the time they're just being smart-arses so it's not worth talking to them on any level as I don't believe that they are worth my time.

When any of my staff hear this happening, often they get more upset about it than me and sometimes they want to make a big deal out of the situation, in my defence. But I tell them "just forget about it" and I talk to them after the bus goes." I tell my staff, "We have much better things to do than give people that want to be mean the attention they don't deserve." I try to lighten things up for my staff and say, "I'm glad these people don't need to go to Specsavers (optical retail chain) as clearly their eyesight is fine!"

I'm not suggesting that you accept bullying in any cases, but now that I'm much older, sometimes I just let stupid comments fly past and refuse to let them get to me.

DON'T ALWAYS EXPECT DIFFERENT RESULTS

> *"If you want different results, you have to try different approaches."*
> **Albert Einstein**

SERVING AND DESERVING

You must learn to take what some people say with a 'grain of salt' because if you don't, people will get under your skin every day and you are the one that suffers. Remember my 'vegies' story? Sometimes your energy is better spent on focusing on you which means not focusing on others. You can't expect to change everyone's mindsets all the time, and you can't be using all your time and energy trying to do that. There are important things in life to get on with.

Many people come and go in my life (tourists, customers, people just passing through) and I know that I will probably never set eyes on them again therefore, it's not worth wasting my valuable time and knowledge helping all the smart-arse ones who don't understand the damage they can do to someone's life by being mean.

Learning when and where to spend your time and energy on trying to change people's behaviour is a necessary skill that requires resilience. Keep the main focus on your close environment. It's best to spend your energy on people that are much more involved in your daily life: people that you see regularly, people in your community, and people that care.

Where is your energy currently being spent? Worrying about what other people think, or on improving your mindset and nurturing relationships with people who are part of your life?

....

....

....

....

....

....

....

....

....

....

What ways can you remain centred and not buy into the drama of others?

....

....

....

....

....

....

....

....

....

What can you do when you feel uncomfortable?

....

....

....

....

....

....

....

....

....

....

WORKING WITH OTHERS

Regardless of what happens in life, you will always have to deal with other people. Whether you go to school or leave school, or go to university or join the workforce — you are faced with countless different personalities you may not have experienced before.

You may one day be working with someone who is two generations older than you, and while they may seem out of touch and set in their ways, they are a great source of personal experience they can share with you. Back when I started working, the older generations used to call people 'love' instead of your name, and back then it was a term of endearment.

Or you may study or work with others from different cultures and have English as their second language. They may have different customs to what you're used to.

Learning to communicate and deal with people from all walks of life is one of the best skills you can develop. It's a life skill that you can take anywhere. Practice it every day and it will help you as well as others. Because as I said, you'll have to learn how to deal with people no matter what.

Doing what you love not only helps others in your community... you also grow. When you are happy doing what you enjoy, it's infectious — it not only lifts up your mood, it lifts the mood of others, and you are inspired to be greater.

If you're not already, where can you get out and join others in your community (sports, drama, dance, volunteer) doing what you love?

....

....

....

....

....

....

....

How does it feel to help others?

....

....

....

....

....

....

....

....

Ask yourself: what else can I add to my life to love it even more?

....

....

....

....

....

....

....

....

....

....

Chapter 10

KEEPING IT REAL DOWN THE LINE

"When you are able to let go of pain and hurt, you can then grow."

Angie Clucas

FOCUS ON THE PRESENT

> "Any man who can drive safely while kissing a pretty girl is simply not giving the kiss the attention it deserves."
>
> Albert Einstein

I have been lucky enough to be asked to be a bridesmaid twice in my life: first, by my best friend and then by my little sister, both occasions for which I felt very honoured. But as much as it was nice to be asked, these particular events were very challenging for me.

The two weddings were many years apart: one when I was a young teenager, the other when I was almost forty years old. But even though there was a big time-lapse between the two, unfortunately, the issues I had as a teen bridesmaid were still the same as an adult.

As much as I wanted to be part of both of these people's special days, it was very tough for me to deal with having to get my dresses made. Because of my size and build, they both needed massive amounts of changes to make mine look the same as the other bridesmaid's dresses. This was not only difficult but expensive, and very time consuming. But hard as that part of the process was, this was not my only major challenge.

At my best friend's wedding (when I was a teen), the bride's little sister was the flower girl, and she was a little bit bigger than me. Then, at my sister's wedding (when I was nearly forty), the flower girl was my daughter who then, was only a little bit smaller than me! I couldn't help thinking that if this wedding had taken place in another year or so, my daughter would have been the same size as me.

BALANCING LOVE AND SH*T

I don't wear dresses because they don't make adult dresses to fit me. When dresses do fit me, they are made for young girls to wear, not adult women. And to have clothes made for you from start to finish is a very expensive exercise.

Weddings, and the types of special occasions where I have a key visible role, make me feel very uncomfortable because I feel that my stature is highlighted and there is no way for me to publicly control the situation. I know that, for example, even when I'm part of a bridal party, I will always have to stand at the end of the line in photos because otherwise, the pictures will look unbalanced and that's the last thing I would want: to make the photos of their special day look silly. I know that these thoughts are all in my head but sometimes it's harder to deal with feelings like this when it involves the people that mean the most to you.

In my case, these people that don't see my stature as an issue: they understand that sometimes they just have to make a few changes so that I can be included and believe me, I am very grateful for that. But in some ways, the issues around my stature can be harder to deal with on special occasions when I'm with the people who are closest to me. These are the times when I really don't have the answers to deal with issues that arise around my height.

And then...

After the photos as the night goes on there is the dance floor. Yep, this is another situation that is very uncomfortable — for both myself and the poor bugger that has to dance with me — because they've probably have never found themselves in this position before!

I find myself stressing out and having a lot of inner issues on days like these. I always try to help make a special day run smoothly for family and friends but at the same time I have to deal with these sticky situations. I don't want issues around my shortness to become a feature of their special day. On these occasions, I don't let on to anyone else what I'm dealing with inside because the people I would normally talk to are the very same ones sharing this big day. Weddings can be stressful, even at the best of times, and I have no intention of putting any more stress on their plates. It's a day to celebrate and be happy.

JUST BEING HONEST

There are not many things that fit into the category of 'not unusual events' that I find hard to deal with but honestly, being in a wedding party is one of them. Without making a big deal out of this problem, I will share this perspective with you: I find that when the topic of me and my stature is talked about, is when I'm not around; so if a situation builds up at a special event where me and my height are the subject of hidden conversations, it hurts and is damaging. This happens because people don't know how to discuss issues that may affect the feelings of someone they love.

The lesson to be learnt from this is that sometimes it's the people you're closest to who have trouble dealing with how to include you in sticky or difficult conversations at certain times, without hurting your feelings. In these close environments, even when the topic is obvious, there can be moments where they don't even know how to bring it up with you. And then you find it awkward to talk to them about these things as well because on any other day, the topic is a non-issue.

There are times when you can't change things and it's nobody's fault. At these times, you just have to live through the moment knowing that it is only a moment in time, and that it will pass. Remembering too, that sometimes you just have to accept that you will have to deal with stuff in life and there's no one to blame because it's no one's fault. It just is. So, I guess what I'm trying to say is be brave enough to work out when you need to "build a bridge and get over it", otherwise life will consume you with shit that doesn't really matter at the end of the day.

Think of a time where someone had difficulty expressing their feelings to you, afraid they'd hurt you? What can you say to create a space for them to express themselves?

....

....

....

....

....

....

....

....

....

....

What can you say to another that creates a safe space for **YOU** to express yourself?

....

....

....

....

....

....

....

....

Is there a situation that is better for you to accept as a rare occasion? (like my wedding example).

....

....

....

....

....

....

....

....

....

HANDLING MY 'STUFF'

Around the time my daughter was getting close to starting school, I began to experience some very strong feelings around how she was going to cope.

Silvia didn't have my condition and was a totally normal girl, but I thought about what others would say when they saw that I was her mum. I was very concerned that the other children would give her a hard time because of my stature and thought of her suffering from being teased at school, even though it had nothing to do with her, disturbed me.

I knew though, that these thoughts were all in my head, so I didn't talk about them to anyone; especially Silvia as that wouldn't have been fair. My anxiety was all about me: she didn't have any fear of having to deal with being teased at school about me because she hadn't even started school yet. *She wouldn't have any idea about what's coming*, I thought, *and it's got nothing to do with her, it's all about me.* I felt bad for her, fearing what I was sure would happen, and I felt it was my fault: any issues that would be coming her way about me were my fault. I didn't want her to suffer. It was really stressing me out.

I remember the day she started school: I was one of those over-protective mums and had great trouble letting her go — to see her walk into the school classroom on her first day — just like all the other parents and kids. But while Silvia was walking beside me, all happy to finally be at 'big' school, I was a nervous wreck, on the inside at least. I didn't know any of the other parents or their children, and this made it feel even harder as I had to deal with my fears as a mum without any way of checking on her except on my own. I didn't know how I was going to come out of my daughter's first week at school in one piece not knowing how she was going to deal with this major event in her life. These feelings and thoughts were overwhelming, even though I knew I was reliving my own experience at school, not hers.

As we entered the front door of her classroom, I could see the shock on the faces of the other adults when they worked out that I was the mother of a child that was going to be a classmate of their children. But, to my surprise, one of them smiled at me and introduced herself and her child to us. I smiled back and shook hands with her and in return, introduced myself and Silvia. The two children started to chat and within minutes, before I realised the bell was ringing, it was time to go into class.

The teacher (who was in her final year of teaching and was very experienced), could sense my anxiety and said, "Would you like to stay a while?" Then, before I had time to think, I found myself sitting at the back of the room near the mat that the children were sitting on. After a short story had been read to the children, the teacher invited all remaining adults to the staff room for a coffee and chat so that we could get to know each other.

This exercise turned out to be very helpful as we all started introducing ourselves and it gave us all a chance to get to know one another. It also gave me an opportunity to share with them a bit about me, and my fears about Silvia potentially getting teased about me. As a result, I was able to explain to them why I was so small and that I hoped that all the other children wouldn't tease my daughter about me. I left the school grounds feeling a little better as all the parents that I had spoken to seemed to understand my concerns. They said that they would shut down anything wrong that was said about me at home.

All day I couldn't concentrate on anything except how my little girl was dealing with all the questions about me that she might be asked by her classmates. I was so anxious to be there for her; I think I was the first parent there to pick my daughter up. I just needed to be there when she came out of the classroom, as all I was thinking about was what I was going to have to deal with when she finished school that day.

LIVE IN THE MOMENT

The school bell rang, and all the children came out each proudly holding a picture that they had drawn in class on their first day. And with them, out came little Silvia, to my huge surprise with a big smile on her face and not a care in the world it seemed! I was so relieved but still concerned and wanted to make sure nothing bad had happened during the day.

> *"I never think of the future —*
> *it comes soon enough."*
> **Albert Einstein**

When we were alone in the car, I started with, "How was your day?"

She replied, "Great Mum, but..."

"But!" my alarm bells rang, *But what?...oh no, here it comes!* I braced myself for the bad news I'd been expecting all along. My fears coming true. What was I going to do? But I didn't want to say anything yet, as she continued, "...but my teacher made me wear my shoes all day. I wasn't allowed to take them off once!"

I laughed out loud, probably louder than what made sense as she didn't know what I'd been thinking. What a great relief! And at that instance I figured out that all my worrying was in my head; my issues where no one else's, expect my own. I had created a day from hell in my head that didn't even exist.

From that day on I was able to be my daughter's mum, and not that terrified child that I had been on my own first day at school. I was able to control myself and not make a big deal out of my feelings of fear, which after it was all over, became laughing points to me. The whole thing was my issue and I'm glad I was able to protect my child from it. She didn't need to be dumped on or involved.

"Stop your fears and issues being passed down to the next generation."

Angie Clucas

Where have you worried so much it consumed you (you made it bigger than it was)? When you finally went through the experience, what was the outcome and how did you feel afterwards?

....

....

....

....

....

....

....

Have there been any recent incidents where an upcoming event reminded/pulled you into the emotion of a past experience? What did you do to move through it?

....

....

....

....

....

....

....

Go back to a past experience where you weren't in control. Knowing what you know now, how would you respond to a situation where you did not feel in control? How would you move through it?

....

....

....

....

....

....

....

Take a look at your vision board — are there any words that you can add to it i.e. resilience, perseverance, worry-free, go-getter, confident, kind? You vision board is a living board — as you continually change, remember to update your board.

INTEGRITY IN AND OUT

Integrity is about 'being true to your word' and having your own good guiding principles to live by. Remember at the beginning of this book when we made 'Rules To Live By'? Living by a good moral compass is having integrity. Making good decisions based on honesty and ethics is integrity.

I like to think of integrity as "walking your truth". Walking your talk. It means that I don't say one thing then act the complete opposite. Things like peer pressure and other people influencing you can make you want to drop your integrity but it takes much more courage to stay true to your own principles regardless of what people say. Showing your integrity can come in many forms, sometimes big, sometimes small, but it's always meaningful. It can feel easier to give in and do what others think you should do but integrity takes courage to stick with your principles and do what you think is the right thing in your own heart.

This is an example of someone that did just that:

One day, in year 7 of school (at about 11 years old), a girl that we will call Jackie decides that for the next year from this day until 365 days later she will not eat McDonalds under any circumstances.

Jackie's first big challenge came on the school camping trip when the bus stopped at McDonalds for lunch on the way to their camping site. Jackie noticed that across the road from McDonalds, there was another shop that looked to her like they'd sell much healthier food. So, she asked the teacher if she could go across the road to buy her lunch as she would not be eating McDonalds. Jackie was showing her integrity by finding a solution to her problem and not just getting McDonalds because everyone else was.

During the school holidays, Jackie came up with the same problem again when she was at the airport. Because the flight they were going on was late at night, McDonalds was the only food place open. But true to her word, she told her mother that she was not going to eat McDonalds. She asked her mother to respect the decision that she had made many weeks ago and to understand why she would not be eating the same food as the rest of the family tonight.

Jackie then asked her mum if she could go to the newsagent at the airport so that she could get a snack to fill her up enough until there was other food available to them. Jackie's Mum said that she was very proud of her for sticking to her word and staying strong about something that was important to her. Keeping her word while achieving a goal. Jackie felt supported and learnt that she could always find a solution to any situation she found herself in and that being able to uphold your integrity shows great character.

UPGRADING TO GREATER

I believe that if we work on improving ourselves and learn how to think positively and boost our own self-esteem then we automatically "upgrade" our lives to something greater. This is what happened to me. I am always striving to live authentically, to treat people with respect and try to help others. It's important to search for things that inspire you and help you become greater. Some things are 'inner things' like learning resilience and being kind, other things are 'outer things' like doing hobbies that you love or learning a new skill. No matter what you do it all happens on 'the inside' because you are the one experiencing it. Throughout this whole book I have been trying to help you 'Upgrade to Greater': to build a vision for your life and live your life on your terms.

Upgrading to Greater is all about taking small steps in the right direction — up your Ladder of Life. The direction of your own dreams and goals.

It can be good to make a list of goals (stepping stones) you want to achieve. It's good to map out your plan for the future you want to create. You can write some goals and experiences you want to have in the future.

This Month

....

....

....

....

....

....

Six Months

....

....

....

....

....

....

1 year

....

....

....

....

....

....

5 years

....

....

....

....

....

....

UPGRADE TO GREATER: START SIMPLE

You can take simple and easy actions that compound over time to make huge leaps and bounds in your personal growth.

Examples of things you can do are:
- Read or listen to self-help books (knowledge is power); learn a new skill (i.e. coding, photography, yoga, etc.).
- Put an inspiration board on your wall next to your vision board. Fill this with quotes that spur you into action.
- Revisiting your values and updating your vision board every year.
- Stop comparing yourself to others.
- Join activities you enjoy that you can do with others — sport, dance, drawing, learn a language (for that future dream holiday on your board). Get out of your comfort zone and join a team where you know no one and make new friends.
- Catching and stopping the negative self-talk.
- At the end of every day reflect and think of 3 things you are grateful for, big or small.
- Smiling with your eyes and from your heart.
- Find friends who 'get' you, just the way you are!
- Volunteer for a cause that is important to you (i.e. animals, homelessness, disability, etc.).

- Choose to face your biggest fear, break it down into small steps, and take action!

What 3 things can you do on a daily or weekly basis to upgrade the quality of your life?

....

....

....

....

....

....

....

How will you know these changes have expanded your life i.e. you feel happier, you've made new friends, your enjoying team sport and exercise, the negative self-talk has stopped.

....

....

....

....

....

....

....

....

....

WHERE ARE YOU NOW?

Have you made any changes while reading this book? What have they been?

....

....

....

....

....

....

....

....

Write where you are in your journey right now. What are you committed to changing or improving in the next six months?

....

....

....

....

....

....

....

....

....

Do a review. Did you make these changes? How did it change you?

....

....

....

....

....

....

....

....

....

CONCLUSION

At some point we all must stop and take a breath. Pull over to the side of your journey and look at how far you have come.

I had a rough start to life.

When we are born, we are all given a name by our parents. This becomes our identity. We have no control over what we are going to look like or which family we are born into. Lucky for me, I was born into a family that understood how to bring me up to deal with the issues that I had to deal with in life.

Just because I'm not so-called 'normal' in appearance, it doesn't mean that I am any less of a human being than others.

I had to think a little differently and grow up mentally at a much younger age than my peers because of how I got treated on a daily basis.

My school experiences made me understand that it was my responsibility to learn how to deal with the issues I faced around others; pointing and calling me names, pushing me around. They had no understanding that their actions would cause damage to the person that was on the receiving end.

It is everyone's responsibility to teach others that taking ownership of their actions can make this world a better place.

It only takes one choice to have a better life. The choice is yours.

I CHOOSE TO LIVE MY LIFE FROM THE INSIDE TO HELP ME DEAL WITH LIFE ON THE OUTSIDE.

WHERE AM I NOW?

Living my best life! Here I am enjoying life with my future husband Gary, my daughter Silvia and her best friend Crystal.

PERMISSIONS

Thank you to ABC News and Croc Candy for use of their work and/or images.

ACKNOWLEDGEMENTS

I would like to thank my Mum, Linda, and my Dad, Murray — without their support over my life and their foresight to raise me like any normal person in order to help me deal with all the issues that I have had to face from looking physically different to most people — I will be forever grateful.

My brother Andrew and my sister Christine, for always being there when I need someone to talk to. I couldn't have asked for a better brother and sister. Thank you.

I also wish to thank my friends that have always stood by me in some of my most challenging times.

My thanks also goes to my godparents Jim and Kath Allison, for helping me to start my new life in Australia and always having my back.

A very big thank you to my partner Gary Downey, for always being my best mate and understanding who I am on the inside — which is something that I will always cherish.

My daughter Silvia for making me so proud of the amazing adult you have grown into, and for also being one of my best friends who is always there for me.

The Dean Publishing team and the Dean family who have become my friends over the last few years. I wish to thank Susan Dean so much because without her this journey would have never happened. Susan showed me that I do have a story to share and I can help others that have issues around being bullied. Thank you also to Matt Jasper for all his help producing my videos and your support every step of my journey.

I would also like to thank Joanne Walters for her support with building my website *Standing Tall from the Inside* and her continual help with Facebook. She always helps me whenever I ask, and nothing is ever too much trouble. For all her help, and friendship, I am and always will be very grateful.

A big thank you to all those people that made my life full of issues, all those bullies who made my life very tough — without you I would not have grown into the strong, considerate character that I am today. I, Angie Clucas am the author of this book, because I have learned so many lessons from people trying to make me feel small and not worth anything...but guess what? You lose and I believe that I won, because I am an honourable and respected person in this world, because you all made me strong enough to **Stand Tall From the Inside**.

ABOUT THE AUTHOR

A ngie Clucas is a speaker, author, manager, anti-bullying advocate and extremely proud mother. Despite being born with a Russell-Silver syndrome, a medical condition that affects normal growth, Angie never let her condition stop her from living her best life.

Challenged by relentless bullying throughout her life, Angie discovered inner resources and deeper ways to overcome the torment. She found ways to rise above the bullies and become her best self.

She has written a chapter about her personal experiences in her first publication, *Resilience: Building a Powerful Mindset.*

Standing Tall From the Inside expands on her knowledge and gives the reader deep insights and wisdom about how to build self-esteem, self-confidence and not let the bullies win. She reveals personal memories and helps the reader find a new perspective on life.

Angie has spoken on stage at Melbourne's Ignite conference, sharing her story and empowering others to stand up for what is right — asking them to be kind instead of callous.

Angie inspires young people all over Australia and the world to **Stand Tall from the Inside!** She is down-to-earth, compassionate and friendly, and also deeply determined to make a change in the lives of others. Her dream is that one day…no child, no teenager, no person will be bullied. And the only way to stop that is through education and kindness.

For more about Angie go to: **standingtallfromtheinside.com**

CPSIA information can be obtained
at www.ICGtesting.com
Printed in the USA
BVHW091412231120
593971BV00002B/260